THOMAS CARNDUFF:
Life and Writings

THOMAS CARNDUFF:
Life and Writings

edited and introduced by
JOHN GRAY

1994
Lagan Press/
Fortnight Educational Trust
Belfast

Published by
Lagan Press
PO Box 110, Belfast BT12 4AB

The publishers wish to acknowledge the financial assistance
of the Cultural Traditions Group in the production of this book.

© Introduction and notes, John Gray
Text of biography and other writings
the estate of Thomas Carnduff, 1994

The moral right of the editor
and estate of the author has been asserted.

A catalogue record of this book is available from the British Library

ISBN No: 1 873687 10 9
Editor: John Gray
Title: Thomas Carnduff: Autobiographical Writings
Format: Paperback (136 mm x 210 mm)
1994

Front Cover Painting: Portrait of Thomas Carnduff by William Conor (????)
(Courtesy of the Ulster Museum and the estate of William Conor)
Cover Design by Chris Best
Set in 10/13.5 Palitino
Printed by Noel Murphy Printing, Belfast

This book is dedicated to all my friends—both old and new—who have assisted in my search for my father's works.

—Noel Carnduff

Acknowledgements

The publishers and editor would like to thank the following for their help and preparation of this publication: Noel Carnduff, Eamonn Mc Kinley, Damian Smyth, Chris Best and the staff of the Linen Hall Library.

Contents

Introduction by John Gray   11
The Autobiography of Thomas Carnduff   57
Other Autobiographical Writings   119

Introduction

It was November 1930. The young Ruddick Millar, an *Irish News* journalist, and himself a minor poet and playwright, found his way to Thomas Carnduff's "little kitchen house" at 7 Hanover Street, off the Old Lodge Road. He was to write the first published profile of his friend, the unemployed "shipyard poet". It was a favour well-justified by the news that the Ulster Repertory Theatre had accepted Carnduff's play, *Workers*, for performance.

Millar found Carnduff "with his sleeves rolled up pounding away at his typewriter", and at work on "an autobiographical novel". Perhaps, at this time, Carnduff envisaged writing in the tradition of Patrick Magill's *Children of the Dead End* or Robert Tressel's *Ragged Trousered Philanthropists*. It is, in any case, the first mention of an autobiographical intention that was to have an extraordinarily long and chequered career.

Indeed, as far back as 1903, when aged 17, Carnduff had kept diaries. Small fragments only have re-surfaced in articles of reminiscence. The notion of an autobiographical novel seems to have died an early death but, by August 1942, he was writing to his second wife, Mary, to tell her "I am going ahead with the auto-bio at a good speed". By October, the future of what was now straightforward biography seemed assured. Richard Rowley (G.V. Williams) and proprietor of the Mourne Press wrote to Mary Carnduff:

> Tom's typescript of the biography came safely to hand and I have read it through more than once. It's fine stuff and I shall be proud to publish it. Will you tell Tom that I'll prune a little, very carefully, and then hand the book over to the printer. I've asked Willie Conor to make me a little drawing of Tom to be used as frontispiece to the book.

War-time paper shortages and Rowley's increasing ill-health may have intervened but, in the event, hopes from this quarter were dashed. It was not until the 1950s that Carnduff appears to have revived interest in the project, and again success seemed imminent. In 1954, he even received an advance of £25 from Cahill & Company of Dublin "on Peadar O'Donnell's suggestion". The publishers do not appear to have had the typescript in their possession, because they merely understood from O'Donnell that the work "is in advance state of preparation".

John Sayers, editor of the *Belfast Telegraph*, certainly did see the completed work because, in August 1954, he wrote saying "spent several enjoyable evenings reading your MS which I found most evocative, and in the concluding chapters very stimulating", and he went on to offer to publish extracts.

By this stage, the work even had a title, *North of the Éire Border*, but, somewhere along the line, the typescript was lost and, with Carnduff's own death in 1956, remained unpublished in his lifetime. A number of drafts of parts of the work survived, and Desmond Greaves of the Connolly Association serialised edited sections in the *Irish Democrat*, between March and May 1958, under the very different title 'Orange Republican Memoirs of Thomas Carnduff'. Greaves appears to have returned the sections of the typescript available to him to the Linen Hall Library, and it was from this source that some chapters were published in full in 1978 in *Irish Booklore* as 'Thomas Carnduff, 1886–1956: Chapters from an Unpublished Autobiography'.

The story of Carnduff's autobiography was not an isolated misadventure. During the 1930s, his plays *Workers*, *Traitors* and *Machinery* were all professionally performed in Belfast and Dublin and yet—until recently—were completely lost. Thus, in an era in which much rhetorical use was made by politicians in particular of the concept of 'the Protestant democracy', the most articulate creative voice of that democracy was effectively buried.

Carnduff was at pains to establish his position within a tradition of working-class writing. He had "made a practice of collecting the biographies of every known working man that Ulster has produced in the past one hundred and fifty years, of which there are some thirty", but it was a tradition that had largely died with the handloom weavers, such as his particular models—"Jimmy Hope, James Orr and Francis Davis". In his own time, St. John Ervine came from humble origins in Ballymacarrett, and provided Ulster drama with its first working-class play, *Mixed Marriage*, set against the background of the 1907 dock strike, but Ervine soon proved much more at home with Presbyterian shopkeepers or village life. Otherwise, Carnduff apart, silence reigned.

For this reason alone, his autobiography is a significant document. Fortunately in recent years his son Noel has tracked down two additional chapters. Annoying gaps remain—nothing on early childhood, a gap between 1914 and 1930 and, hence, nothing on the First World War, the troubles of the 1920s, his service in the 'C' Specials, and little on his role as 'shipyard poet'. Another apparent gap relates to the Young Ulster Society. Again, thanks largely to Noel Carnduff, we now have resources with which to fill most of the gaps. Well over a hundred newspaper articles, many of them autobiographical in nature, have come to light, as have two sets of correspondence, including an extensive series of letters to his second wife Mary and covering the years 1941 to 1943. Much of the text of the known missing plays has been located, and others previously unknown have surfaced.

Thus, while it remains best to publish the autobiography as found—that is, in incomplete form—it is now possible to complement it with a full essay of introduction, albeit one concentrating on those aspects of his life not covered in the autobiography.

For some, this may serve to confuse the issue—it will become readily apparent that Carnduff was not a socialist, not an Orangeman in any straightforward or conventional mould, and not a Republican, at least in any 20th-century sense. The actual complexities of the road he sought to pursue make him a more, rather than less, interesting person.

***

As a child, Carnduff was witness to the breakneck growth of the city in the late Victorian and early Edwardian period, and the transfer of the Carnduff family from the rural environment of Ballyauglis, near Drumbo in Co. Down, to Sandy Row was still well-recalled:

> It was during the fifties and sixties of the last century that the inhabitants of the rural areas adjoining commenced their influx into the industrial centres. Streets of small kitchen houses so familiar to Belfast were springing up like mushrooms in the Sandy Row area.
> Families from outlying districts would pile their belongings on to a country cart coming into town—for railway travel was beyond the pocket of those country folk—and unloaded at the first working-class area they came to, hoping that all would be well with them. There was work in the mills, factories and shipyards and, to them, higher wages than the land could possibly offer.
> Sandy Row was Eldorado to these folks from Lambeg, Lisburn,

Hillsborough and Dromore. They would travel all night, and probably land in Belfast on a bleak, frosty morning, before an empty house in one of the back streets of that district. All they could hope for was a kindly welcome.

It was in 1861 that my grandfather left his cottage in Drumbo, joined the stream and settled in No. 18 Sandy Row. In my early years in Sandy Row, practically every family residing there had connections with the country.

Carnduff himself, though born after the death of his grandfather in 1882, fondly remembered, almost as a point of pilgrimage, "the row of one-storied white-washed cottages which stretched from the corner of Hope Street right up to No. 22, where my grandfather lived for many years".

His father, James Graham Carnduff, had left Drumbo by a very different but common enough route. Born in 1843, he had enlisted in the Royal Horse Artillery at the age of 17. Although he appears to have been too young to have served in the Indian Mutiny, at least one family connection must have done so, as a mutiny service medal remains in the family's possession. By 1867, James Carnduff was enjoying a home posting as a corporal based at Newbridge, County Kildare, where some of his work, whether officially or unofficially, was as "an army school master". Here he married Mary Melville and three children followed. After the early death of his wife, he married for a second time to Jane Bollard and a further seven children arrived, of whom Thomas Carnduff was the youngest and the only one born in Belfast.

The circumstances of the return to Belfast were difficult, as his father, now describing himself as a 'labourer', had been afflicted with blindness and invalided out of the army on "a meagre pension" of ninepence a day, and Carnduff's mother died soon, in 1891, when he was five. Disability and premature death of parents threatened children with penury in pre-welfare state Belfast. As late as 1907, Carnduff attended an Ulster Hall rally in support of improved pensions for army veterans.

The family found a tenuous foothold in Little May Street in the Cromac area, a melting pot for poorer working-class families:

> Cromac Street at that period was a mixed locality. Little May Street, Hamilton Street, and Henrietta Street were inhabited in the main by Protestant families. A number of my father's relatives lived there. I attended a Protestant infant school at the corner of Eliza Street,

which, if my memory serves me, was named Haslett's School. Afterwards most of these families moved to 'The Plains' when that district became a built up area.

Other circumstances indeed suggest poverty, a diet in which "porridge, broth, stew, potatoes and buttermilk, without variation, was the daily circumstances"—they lived in the gasworks district and could not afford gas. And yet this was not quite the conventional poor, unskilled, working-class home, nor could it be, with books on the shelves, and a blind father who liked having "Byron and Shelley" read to him. There were even, at one time, the accoutrements that only money could buy—with "Edison Bell records on the phonograph", scratched though they might be. It was, however, at best, an unstable beginning.

Change, too, was affecting almost every element of Carnduff's childhood environment:

> I saw the last of the Cromac Water carts, with its horse drawn container, selling water in the streets at so much a bucket. Occasionally a herd of nanny goats would be driven through the streets whilst their owners ladled out pure fresh milk at a penny a time.

And the same was true in the city centre, which was close by:

> I can still visualise the old White Linen Hall in the glory of a summer's day, with its cool and shady grounds festooned with stately foliage, jealously watching the inevitable destruction of what was at one time the aristocratic residential quarter of the city—we children, had fun and frolics round the railed enclosure of the old building.

The White Linen Hall was demolished to make way for the City Hall in 1896. Closer to home, the Chapel Fields, bordered by Ormeau Avenue and stretching from Joy Street to Linen Hall Street, was the principal playground:

> A venue for football fans and, during the festive seasons, they were crammed with roundabouts, circuses, wild beast shows, and boxing booths. I remember some wild scenes here when the crowd got out of hand and the showmen had to defend their property with whatever weapons they could fashion.

The Fields was soon to vanish and even the place names of Carnduff's childhood were rapidly overtaken by events:

In my boyhood days, Donegall Road was always referred to as the 'The Blackstaff'. Durham Street was 'Pound Loney'. 'Bowers Hill', now the Shankill Road. Ballynafeigh was known to us as 'The Brickfields'.

This childhood and adolescent image of Belfast as a dynamic and rapidly developing city was to remain with Carnduff through the far bleaker inter-war years, but another contrasting image was to endure: in the autobiography, he refers to "the glamour of Phoenix Park" seen from the Royal Hibernian Military School which he attended from 1896 to 1900. In those years, he "often roamed the streets of Dublin, staring with a northerner's awe at the ancient and historic buildings and broad majestic thoroughfares. I may have wondered why my own city could never capture the proud, almost regal atmosphere which great capitals retain through the centuries".

Childhood wonder at the breakneck rate of change in his home city of Belfast was soon tempered by the struggle to make a living. Although his family lacked the cohesiveness of others, it is remarkable how important family connections remained, even for him, in getting a start in the hard world of unskilled and semi-skilled labour. Getting a start did not protect him from being used as "a beast of burden". Although the Edwardian era was, in many respects, the heyday of the city's expansion, Carnduff was quite correct in suggesting that "the labouring class was bordering on starvation" in an environment in which the differential between skilled and unskilled wage rates was the greatest in the British Isles. Added to the insecurity caused by low wages was the instability of employment itself with marked recessions in 1904/5 and 1908. Although a disproportionately high percentage of Catholics was unskilled workers, the majority of those afflicted by such conditions was Protestant, like Carnduff.

Unskilled and poorly paid he may have been, but, as a single male, he enjoyed some disposable income. In a fragment of diary for March 1905, we find him paying 19s. 6d. for a suit and going to the Theatre Royal, although even then aware of his limited means—"saw a few of the town's big-wigs in the grand circle. The seats are very expensive in the circle—one shilling each. I suppose the big-wigs have pots of money to spend". Big-wigs and the working-class inhabitants of the pit like Carnduff got a good grounding in melodramatic excess:

> The play this week is *The Face at the Window*. We are held spellbound with three murders, and the detective brought to life through some electric contraption, long enough to write down the name of the murderer before he returns to his heavenly abode.

Elsewhere, he records that "he spent many enjoyable nights in theatreland up to the outbreak of the Great War", remembering the great touring companies of the time with J. Forbes Robertson in Hamlet, Fred Benson's company and Sir Henry Irving in the dramatic version of *Faust*.

Hard though his early working experiences were, some offered encouragement to extend the interest in reading which stemmed from his father. Here and there, the literate tradition of the hand loom weavers survived. Thus, for a brief period, he worked alongside hacklers in a linen mill, or 'hecklers' as they were known, thus characterised because of their argumentative ways, encouraged by the practice of "setting aside one 'berth' at their bench for a 'reader' ... [who], instead of working at his trade read the morning newspapers to his comrades". Then, at the *Ulster Echo*, he "mixed with compositors and printers who were well read and above the average intelligence, and so I was forced to study books and periodicals to keep pace with the conversation". By this stage, he had no doubt discovered the public library in Royal Avenue.

With his Sandy Row and staunch Orange background, the direction of his first involvements on the political and cultural battlefields of the city was naturally determined. He gives us the only known insider's account of sectarian gang warfare at the time of the Boer War, and, returning from the Royal Hibernian Military School with a "strong Dublin accent", may have had to prove himself all the more in the field.

An obvious and associated rite of passage was the flute band. Writing in *The Bell* in 1942, he offered interesting comment on the bands of the day—"There were no accordion bands in the city. I don't even remember the existence of a pipe band. There were a number of brass and reed bands, and dozens of fife-and-drum combinations who played more by luck than tuition". He turned to the latter:

> I became a member of ... [the] Britannic Star Flute Band. After several months practice, we managed four party tunes. We usually spent our Easter Monday's in a trip to Larne, returning to our rooms via

Wellington Place and Great Victoria Street to Sandy Row. Incidentally, we timed our homeward journey to co-incide with the return of a nationalist band from a Great Northern Railway trip. On two occasions we emerged out of the collision with all our drums burst.

An associated arena was the Custom House steps, then Belfast's Speakers' Corner, and the venue for the inflammatory meetings of Arthur Trew's Belfast Protestant Association. Carnduff may not have been involved in the attack on a Catholic Corpus Christi procession which led to Trew's jailing in 1902, but he, with many others, joined the Belfast Protestant Association soon after.

It was a matter of course that Carnduff would join the Orange Order as did "practically every male belonging to the Protestant industrial classes". As he explains in the autobiography, family involvement meant that it "was in my blood long before I was the age for joining". When the time came, a major schism had occurred in Orange ranks, a split which even caused conflict in the family. Carnduff sided with those who defected to the newly-independent Orange Order and was initiated in 1903. It was a step which Carnduff associates with a radicalising trajectory, culminating in the 'national spirit' of the Magheramorne Manifesto issued at 'The Twelfth' in 1905.

Matters were rather more complex. The initial issue of dispute between the Independents and the official order was the inspection of convent laundries, an issue which owed more to sectarianism than any vague programme of social reform. The conflict came to a head when Thomas Sloan, Trew's successor at the Custom House steps, fought a South Belfast bye-election in 1902 against the Conservative candidate and won. Now, as successor in the seat to the old Orange hero, William Johnston of Ballykilbeg, Sloan was "prepared to go through again the Battle of the Boyne". For this affront to the Orange and Conservative establishment, he was expelled from the official order, and the Independent breakaway followed.

Carnduff was certainly involved at this early stage. Until the issue of the Maghermorne Manifesto, the Independent platform at best combined arguments for Protestant supremacy in all spheres with working-class resentment at their betrayal by the Unionist and Conservative business and landlord class. At this time, the Belfast Protestant Association continued to serve as a political wing of the new order and, in March 1905, thanks to a fragment of diary, we find Carnduff in attendance at an election meeting in Shaftesbury Square.

Nonetheless, Carnduff is right to draw attention to the remarkable nature of the Maghermorne Manifesto. Drawn up by the new Grand Master of the Order, Lindsay Crawford, it contrasted dramatically with all that had gone before. Here was a heartfelt plea for reconciliation between ordinary Catholics and Protestants based on a mutual recognition of common oppression. So unexpected was it, that it was initially simply denounced by the Catholic *Irish News*, and cynically dismissed by some unionists, because it was surrounded by plenty of 'Protestant padding', and yet the new themes it enunciated were to remain in the ascendant within the Independent Order at least until late 1907.

The radical phase of the Independent Order's development was followed by, and in part overlapped with, an upsurge in labour agitation, and Carnduff rightly devotes considerable attention to the great dock strike of 1907—the occasion which caused a Liberal government to send more troops to the city than at any point in the period up to 1914. Although Carnduff was not directly involved as a striker—indeed the newspaper he worked for, the *Ulster Echo*, was amongst those most hostile to the strikers—his participation on the periphery was typical of many unskilled and semi-skilled Protestant workers. His account of how a crowd assembled in Sandy Row at an early stage in the strike, rallying under a Union Jack and "singing Orange songs", and marched off to the docks to attack blacklegs tallies closely with other contemporary sources.

Even at a much later stage when the police had mutinied, and the army opened fire on rioters in the Lower Falls, we find Carnduff and his friend Nugent, like thousands of others, hovering on the edge of the battle, wondering whether to get involved. Again, very typically, two factors dissuaded them: lack of sympathy with the police mutineers most of whom they presumed—as it happens inaccurately—were Catholics, and an assumption that Catholic nationalists had their own agenda in taking on the army. The perception that the Falls riots were the key moment in the breaking of working-class unity in the 1907 strike movement was, however, entirely accurate, as was Carnduff's conclusion that it ended in defeat with "the strikers ... forced back on the masters' terms".

It was a defeat which almost coincided with a growing assault on Lindsay Crawford and the radical and 'national' perspective within the Independent Orange Order, leading to Crawford's expulsion in 1908. Carnduff was not the only person to resign in disgust—a number of lodges did so. Carnduff's reaction was not as dramatic as that of some. Lindsay Crawford emigrated to Canada, became leader of the Irish Determination

League, and first Free State Trade Representative in New York. Richard Braithwaite, one time secretary of the Belfast Protestant Association, was by 1914 sharing a platform with James Connolly to denounce partition. Carnduff, more modestly, was to be found "rejoining the order some years later". It was only 'looking back' from the perspective of the post-war period that he was to recognise fully the "tragedy to our country" represented by the defeat of the thinking reflected in the Magheramorne Manifesto.

Nonetheless, his political disillusion was real enough, and it was to coincide with the harsh economic realities of married life and raising a family. In 1907, he had married Susan McCleery McMeekin and two children followed before the war. In the autobiography, he recounts the inevitable hardship that followed:

> My wages were eighteen shillings a week, so my wife decided to go on working until we managed to collect a home. She was still working eight years after the wedding and Jim and Joe had been added to the family. It was no life for a young woman. We were soon having to struggle to make ends meet.

Understandably, she had little enthusiasm for the political excitements of the day, and was often to look askance at his unremunerative literary aspirations. While in the pre-war period his fevered ransacking of the shelves of the public library was not to bear fruit, he was inevitably drawn back into the anti-Home Rule mobilisation of the Protestant working-class community.

Like other erstwhile Independent radicals, he faced intense pressures in the period up to 1912 to fall in with the unionist anti-Home Rule mobilisation. There was the positive pressure of communal feeling, and there were the negative sanctions against Protestant disloyalists, notably exercised in the shipyard expulsions of 1912. Certainly Carnduff implies, in his account, that it was the positive emotion which moved him.

Yet the course of his mobilisation suggests that earlier resentments between Independents and the Orange and unionist establishment were not entirely forgotten. Thus Carnduff did not initially join the Ulster Volunteer Force, rather he was attracted to the Young Citizen Volunteers (YCV) which he joined in October 1912, one month after their formation.

A crucial distinction between this organisation and that of the UVF was that the YCV were ostensibly 'non-sectarian and non-political'. In some respects they were an élite militia force, with an initial joining fee of 2s. 6d.

and a monthly contribution of 6d., and their own particularly elegant uniforms which the members had to pay for. To some extent, the movement reflected a spirit of civic responsibility and, in 1913, it was proposed that the YCVs place themselves at the disposal of the government.

This overture was spurned and, in any case, many YCV leaders were prominent unionists. As the Home Rule crisis mounted, pressure on the YCVs to merge with the UVF increased, and, in March 1914, the leadership proposed just that. Some YCVs resigned rather than do so, but not Carnduff, who accordingly took part in the April 1914 UVF gun-running operations.

Carnduff's autobiography, at least as it survives, is silent on the First World War and, indeed, till the mid-1920s. Surprisingly, too, his prolific journalistic output casts only limited light on the period. On the outbreak of war, he did not immediately join up:

> When World War I broke out many of my shipyard mates joined up and there was soon a shortage of semi-skilled workers in the yards. I made an application and was granted a hand driller's kit. Most outside boilership work was allocated to repair warships. It was interesting work but the hours were long and the labour rather tedious. Although with overtime and war bonus, we generally managed a wage packet of three or four pounds a week, the hand-driller's basic wage was still as low as twenty five shillings a week. It was my first experience of earning big money, yet with the prices of essential commodities soaring skywards this meant little difference to the workers' standard of living.

Carnduff's delay in joining up was by no means untypical—by January 1916 only 1.6 per cent of the population of Antrim and Down had volunteered. In the same year, the *Belfast Street Directory* first lists the Carnduffs as occupying 7 Hanover Street, to remain the family home till 1944. A small two-up two-down kitchen house, without even access via a back entry, the new address off the Old Lodge Road, and in one of the rougher areas of the city, hardly indicated new found real prosperity.

In any case, Carnduff suggests that finally "the war fever got into my blood" and he joined the Royal Engineers. His first volume of verse, *Songs from the Shipyard* (1924) included 'Messines, 17th July 1917' where he and others "uncowed by hell's artillery, kept faith with country and with God", and in the introduction to the same volume, William Moore includes among the facts that Mr. Carnduff "wishes it to be known" that he "spent three years in France with the Royal Engineers". There remains some inconsistency with his demob papers, which indicate that he joined up as late as 8th September 1917, although he was then to serve until 8th June 1919. Elsewhere he describes "sitting on the Menin Road with every ounce of patriotic zeal scared out of me" and concedes that there was no question of any "mention of distinguished conduct to my army record".

Prior to demobilisation, Workman & Clark had indicated that his position as a hand driller was reserved for him. "It was [but] the following month there was a pay-off in the yard, and for the first time in my life I was on the dole". Initially, the position did not seem absolutely desperate—"being an ex-serviceman with a family, I was supposed to receive preferential treatment. My unemployment allowance was twenty-nine shillings a week. This lasted six months, then you applied for an extended benefit. A family man was generally lucky".

Carnduff was also affected by technological change—"machinery had progressed to such an extent that riveting and hand-drilling was an ancient craft", and eventually he got a new start with the lowlier status of platers' helper, but eleven months later was laid off again. During the 1920s, he was to suffer eleven lay offs concluding with the catastrophe of Workman & Clark's closure, described in his autobiography.

Although Carnduff was never again directly caught up in politics, he clearly supported the foundation of the new Northern Ireland state and was prepared to play his part in its defence in the early troubled years of the 1920s. Although often described as a former 'B' Special, he in fact joined the less well-known 'C1' Specials in February 1922 and served until their abolition in December 1925. Originally the Ulster Special Constabulary included 'A', 'B', and 'C' categories, with 'A' Specials on full time service, 'B' Specials on part time and local service, but with 'C' Specials viewed as a reserve élite.

Colonel Wickham, RUC Commissioner for Belfast, writing in November 1921, saw the formation of the 'C' Specials as a way of dealing with "the growth of unauthorised loyalist defence forces" and "obtaining the services of the best elements of these organisations". He went on to suggest that "the force is intended as a military one only, to be called out in grave emergency to act in a military capacity. They will not of necessity be utilised for local defence but may be drafted to any theatres of operation within the six counties". Carnduff was a relatively late joiner, and may have seen little active service. Towards the end of his life, he was to tell James Kelly of the *Irish Independent* that he joined the Specials "more from adventure than anything else", surely an inadequate explanation.

Outside his USC service, Carnduff must have seen much of the 1920s troubles both in the Old Lodge Road area and in the shipyards. Alas only tantalising references are available. In an *Irish Times* profile published in 1954, readers were told that "his 'behind the scenes' account of regular shipyardmen helping their Catholic fellow-workers to escape across the Lagan, while the real trouble was caused by political gangsters from outside, will some day make dramatic reading". This may well have been a reference to a still missing section of the autobiography. Then again, as we shall discuss later, we find him, in 1940, planning a play set against the same background. The sole extant fragment on the subject is the poem 'The Riot (August, 1921)' which did not appear until the publication of his 1932 volume, *Songs of an Out-of-Work*. Here he contrasts the normal peace of Harkly Street with the moment when "hell has opened its floodgates" and a sniper opens up, but does not elaborate beyond comparing the humanity of the street with the remote and dehumanising forces of violence.

Unemployment had given Carnduff the opportunity to take seriously a fondness he had had for some years of "writing doggerel", and he found a ready if not lucrative market for his output. In 1923, he had 28 poems published, chiefly in the *Belfast Telegraph*, its sister paper, *Ireland's Saturday Night* and in the Presbyterian *Witness*. In the following year, a further 37 appeared, as did his first published volume of verse, *Songs from the Shipyards*.

His was not the only volume of verse with some working-class provenance to appear in Belfast in 1924, which also saw the publication of Harry Midgley's *Thoughts from Flanders*. The future labour leader's poetry was notable for its pre-occupation with the war experience and was marked by a deep religiosity. Carnduff's work, half of which comprised verses already published in the *Belfast Telegraph*, included only four war poems and little of religion, but was principally devoted to a celebration of the shipyards and shipyardmen. There were the bread-and-butter poems, one for every ship launch, with conventional metaphor of "maiden hesitating when her wedding eve is nigh". Then the panegyrics for shipyardmen, "With loyal hearts in time of war, with ready hands in peace", and only occasionally more effective detail as in 'The Scaler':

Looking aslant at your comrade
Scraping the dirt from his eye
Peering above at the hatchways

For a glimpse of the clear blue sky
Chipping and scraping like niggers,
Cleaning what never was clean,
Licking a blood soaked finger,
Leaving the skin on a beam

The comparison with Patrick Magill, 'the navvy poet', was obvious, even if William Moore, in his introduction to the volume, was a little unfair in describing Carnduff's "attempt to imitate him". Less a matter of poetic criticism, but of more contemporary interest, was the sense of doubt that crept in alongside celebration of Belfast's industrial triumph. The shipyardmen had "one resolve, one earnest hope,/Our prestige to regain", and faced those who "With jealousy, cant, and rancour,/They would crush her world-wide fame". In 'The Hungry Folk', they were now those "who struggle 'neath a yoke of hard and bitter times".

Understandably, for a poet who was otherwise unemployed and with a family to feed, Carnduff clearly played his market place, such as it was. Poems which did not appear in the book included 'July 12th 1923', and, in 1924, 'Lord Carson' and 'The Free State Tariff Wall'. These no doubt reflected Carnduff's own allegiances but were, at the same time, commercially timed. When ship launches tailed off in 1924 and 1925, Carnduff found an alternative by tailoring verses about places, many of which he may have known less than well, for almost every Ulster local weekly.

Following the publication of *Songs from the Shipyards*, Carnduff found a new role as the prose voice of the shipyardmen thrown on the dole. In addition to the 32 poems published in 1925, nine articles now appeared, and, in addition to the *Belfast Telegraph*, he now wrote for the *Irish News* and the *Sunday Independent*.

He did so against a background in which early relatively confident assumptions about provision for the unemployed were rapidly shattered. As with very many shipyard workers, he found that successive periods of unemployment exhausted his contribution-based statutory entitlement to benefit. It was a reasonable assumption on his part that, as a Protestant exserviceman and shipyard worker with family, he would receive sympathetic treatment within the discretionary benefit system operated by the Poor Law Guardians, but it was to prove misplaced.

The system was in fact overwhelmed by mass unemployment, first on a short lived basis in the recession of 1924–25, and then more fundamentally in the Great Depression from 1928 onwards. The Poor Law Guardians, mainly Belfast businessmen, were all well aware that their expenditure was a charge on the Belfast rates, which they had a direct interest in keeping low. Carnduff, as with thousands of others, found himself faced with the tyranny of proving willingness to work in a city where no jobs could be found, or of undertaking out-door relief work for benefit in kind, or for rates far below those paid in Britain.

If the previous years were lean, we were now up against the real thing. The Union Workhouse was already overcrowded. Outdoor relief, or, as it came to be popularly called, ODR became an institution. If you had run out of your unemployment benefit, you made application for outdoor relief ... You weren't allowed to earn more than twenty eight shillings in any one week. Instead of being paid in cash, you received a 'chit' for the amount which you presented to your grocer.

Noel Carnduff remembers the consequences at home—"We managed, we were better than some. I never tasted butter or fresh milk until I was 14. Sometimes porridge was the main meal. We did get liver sometimes, but it was liver with those big white veins in it ... a treat was a pennyworth of broken biscuits". Holidays were possible, but only if taken for free, as in a month spent camping on the Cave Hill below the old limestone quarry.

It would be a mistake to assume that Carnduff senior readily adopted socialist solutions to the crisis. Rather, he wrote to the newspapers harking back to an idealised view of the united Ulster of pre-1914 and asking "is it that we have lost the old fighting spirit of the North?". He proposed that they "make every day an Ulster Day" and that government, Chambers of Commerce and the trade unions should join together in an attempt to put Ulster back on its feet".

In this endeavour, he saw betrayal on every side. Thus he was scathing about "most of the clergy", who spent their time "cackling about 'heresy' or the perils of drink to men who wouldn't recognise a pint if they saw one" and who "were more in danger from starvation than thirst at present". He went on to note cynically that "once upon a time it was considered a glorious sacrifice for ministers to suffer with their flock—once upon a time!".

He was not necessarily any more sympathetic to would be reformers "who keep yapping about the poverty of the masses as though they were reduced to animals". Certainly, Carnduff accepted that "poverty is a calamity", but pride required a more positive if unlikely perspective—that such hardship "produces all that is best in man". Enforced leisure certainly enabled him to play an active role on a variety of stages.

We may assume that he had re-joined the Independent Orange Order and, in 1927, we find him playing an active role in the formation of the Independent Literary and Debating Society which met in the Independent Orange Hall in Great Victoria Street. This had as its purpose "inducing the younger members to take a more practical interest in parliamentary, municipal and educational questions of the day".

In 1929, the Society held a mock election debate in which Protestant working-class discontent with the government was evident with Labour winning 70 votes, the Independent 10 votes, and the Conservative three. Carnduff, as the Independent candidate, glorified the Independent role before the war, and viewed Labour as "a foreign element", arguing that "for 100 years they had been bamboozled by the Tory Party, and they were not going to be bamboozled for the next 100 by the Labour Party".

Nor did the nationalist opposition, such as it was, offer any attractions. Speaking at an unemployed meeting in April 1928, Carnduff did indeed say that "the President of the Free State got £700 less than Lord Craigavon, but then people here had the Union Jack, and had to pay for it", but at the same time suggested that "the opposition wanted Stormont Castle at the back of Millfield" and accused them of "getting 18 shillings a week for merely signing their names".

Carnduff's letters to the papers also reflected his burgeoning cultural interests. In 1926, he was announcing the formation of a Poets' Club, later the Belfast Poetry Circle, "organised by a few contributors to the columns of the *Belfast Telegraph*". In further letters, he wrote on 'Ulster Workingmen Poets', showing a good knowledge of the weaver poets and on 'The Poetry of Orangeism'. In both cases he had clearly scoured the shelves of the public library and, in the case of the weaver poets, was seeking to resurrect them three decades in advance of John Hewitt's work. He was soon to lament lack of middle-class support for the Belfast Poetry Circle, and to face criticisms from other correspondents speaking of "the common illiterate herd".

Carnduff was by now in demand as a lecturer—he addressed the Poetry Society on 'Scansion', spoke to the Olive Branch Lodge of the Independent Order of Good Templars on 'Shipbuilding and Shipbuilders', and, perhaps most interestingly, to the Independent Literary and Debating Society on 'Stories from Ulster History'. He opened with the 'Cuchulain or mythical period of Ulster History' and, in a wide ranging survey, devoted considerable attention to the United Irishmen—"the men who lived and died for Ireland's cause in and around what is now her foremost city". While, as early as 1925, he had written for the *Sunday Independent* on 'Rebel Ulster', we need not doubt that speaking on the theme in the Independent Orange Hall, as he was now, he was setting the United Irishmen in the context of the history of the Protestant community.

Another fruitful connection was that with York Street Non-Subscribing Presbyterian Church. Despite his scathing comments on the majority of clergymen, Carnduff remained a believer, and at York Street joined a congregation which, in the Reverend A.L. Agnew, had a minister who, almost uniquely in the Belfast of the 1920s, proclaimed himself a socialist. Carnduff's original contact may have been through the parent church's outlying Stanhope Street Mission, which was close to the Carnduff home in Hanover Street. Apart from religious observance, Carnduff was soon drawn into the wide range of cultural and social activities associated with the church. Thus, in 1926, he recited his poetry to the Church Guild, in 1927 spoke on 'The Romance of Shipbuilding', in 1928 organising an 'Ex-Servicemen's Night', and in 1929 spoke on 'The Humorous Side of Life'.

A more significant development was the formation, apparently sometime in 1929, of an amateur dramatic society, the Stanhope Players. Their first bill included "two short plays", one, *The Jarvey*, by Carnduff's constant associate, Ruddick Millar, and the other Carnduff's own *Politics*. Carnduff's play was set "in the kitchen of a shipyardman's home" and against the background of an imagined election in 1932. Later in the year, the dramatic society, now transmuted into the York Street Dramatic Society, presented another double bill with Carnduff's contribution being a two-act play, *Revolt in Ballyduff*, set in the kitchen of a farmhouse in County Antrim. Ruddick Millar was later to describe these early Carnduff plays as "comedies".

It must have been at about this time that Carnduff, as related in the autobiography, went to hear Richard Rowley speak at the YMCA on 'Drama'. Certainly, at this stage, we should discount Carnduff's autobiographical modesty to the effect that "I had never taken part in a public discussion in my life". The conversation with Rowley, that led to the writing of *Workers*, took place against a background in which Carnduff was already involved in writing for the York Street Players. Carnduff suggests that *Workers* took him four months to write and, indeed, by the end of 1929 Rowley was telling the Elmwood Fellowship that "he had received a beautiful play written by a Queen's Island worker".

In the autobiography, Carnduff suggests that he had already taken another audacious step, and had established his "typewriting agency" at 109 Donegall Street. This was also the address of E.H. Thornton, who had printed *Songs from the Shipyard* in 1924. The terms in which Carnduff advertised his new enterprise certainly suggested extravagant and decidedly unworldly hopes:

> **THOMAS CARNDUFF**
> (The Shipyard Poet and Writer)
> *Will type poems, songs, plays, stories, essays,*
> *lectures, sermons at moderate charges.*
> *Letters and circulars duplicated.*
> *Criticism and help. Call or write.*

As he himself recounts, the business was an unmitigated failure, and worse still, it was to be a full three years before the performance of *Workers*. In the meantime, much of his typing was of his own work and he was more successful with his journalism using personal experience of outdoor relief work in 'With Pick and Shovel: My First Day's Road Job on a Belfast Relief Scheme', and enhancing his reputation as the voice of the worker with a whole series of articles in *Ireland's Saturday Night*, published during 1930, on the lifestyle of various occupations ranging from 'The Charwoman' through 'Here's the Bin Men' and 'The Belfast Carter' to 'The Small Business Man'. For the *Irish Presbyterian* he was to become "the manual workers' representative and friend".

As a poet, he was to enjoy his swansong with *Songs of an Out-of-Work*, published by Quota Press in 1932. Although it appeared after the launch of *Workers*, it is best considered here. While generally these poems were more polished and confident than those of 1924, they remain resolutely, as the *Irish Independent* critic put it, of "the Kipling-Service-McGill school". Although he was later to lament how far local poets had abandoned the local vernacular for English or international models, he himself was strongly influenced in the same way, and did not adopt the dialect of the earlier weaver poets whom he otherwise admired.

Nonetheless, as an increasingly well known local figure, his new volume received substantial and sympathetic coverage and even a review in the *Times Literary Supplement*—"they are good songs, strongly rhythmical and charged with real human feelings". In his foreword, Carnduff suggested that his poems "may seem to have a spice of bitterness in them", but the *Northern Whig* was able to exonerate him. "'Bitterness'" is hardly the word one would choose to characterise what might more justly be described as a consciousness of almost bewildered resentment ... Small trace is there here of the bitterness ... known as 'Bolshevism'". Indeed so, as in 'The Out-of-Works':

> What have we done to you,
> What have we said,
> That you should take from us
> Our daily bread?

How anxiously Carnduff must have watched the fate of *Workers*. Even the patronage of Richard Rowley counted for little in the circumstances of the Ulster theatre at the time, and the autobiography accurately describes the huge difficulties of getting *Workers* performed. While one commentator has suggested some form of continuity in working-class Ulster drama between St. John Ervine, through Carnduff to Sam Thompson, it is truer to say that the first tendency died almost at birth, and that the latter one was so far in the future as to be out of reach—Thompson's *Over the Bridge* was not performed until after Carnduff's death.

Rather, Carnduff was writing for a declining theatre, which amongst other things was dying of caution. Only the faintest embers of the earlier satirical vigour of the Ulster Literary Theatre remained within the now more staidly named Ulster Theatre which still put on its annual short season at the Grand Opera House. That in itself placed huge constraints on what could be performed because, as Carnduff relates, the Warden family acted as ready censors of what was performed there. Censorship could operate by title alone with contents unseen—thus a decade earlier Louis Walsh had had the gravest difficulty in getting a performance of *The Pope at Killybuck*, although it was a light Ulster comedy later popular in amateur circles. Performance at the Empire, owned by the slightly more tolerant Findlater family, was possible, but only under the more innocuous title of *The Auction at Killybuck*.

Clearly, a play baldly entitled *Workers*, with serious purpose, and in Belfast working-class speech employed for the first time in Ulster drama, faced difficulties. Carnduff was fortunate that his problem coincided with the emergence of the Ulster Repertory Theatre led by Richard Hayward and supported by younger actors impatient with the stagnation of the Ulster Theatre. Hayward was no radical, but was an enthusiast for the authentic speech of Ulster. The terms he offered Carnduff, with reduced royalties of five per cent appear niggardly, but he too was taking great risks. Hence, a first performance at the Abbey in Dublin rather than in Belfast. Carnduff served his cause well as self-publicist, telling the *Daily Mail* that "he decided to walk to Dublin" to see his play, but that "some unknown benefactor" had paid his fare. In the event, the play received an enthusiastic reception—the *Irish Independent* went so far as to suggest that "*Workers* has the photographic realism of Sean O'Casey, without that writer's stagecraft, but Mr. Carnduff has distinct possibilities". And yet Carnduff's plot was conventional enough, albeit transmuted to the city setting:

> It is the old 'Triangle' play, with a Sandy Row setting. John Waddell, a very 'coarse' type of shipyardworker, is a drunkard and a wife beater. His wife might have married Jim Bowman, who has spent most of the virtues her husband lacks. Finally she succumbs to Jim's pleading and agrees to go with him but an accident on 'the island' which seriously injures Waddell intervenes, with somewhat conventional psychological reactions.

It was enough to keep the publicity going—thus the *Daily Express* announced "Workless Dramatist Triumphs in the Camp of the 'Enemy'". Carnduff again played his part well—"I was expecting someone to shout 'Up de Valera' and I was prepared, if that happened, to shout 'Up Ulster' and then I suppose the row would be on. But they were great."

More seriously, as in the autobiography, he made no more than a modest claim for his achievement—"for a Belfast working-man like myself to have shown in a theatre with the traditions of the Abbey some of the heroism and humanity of the men with whom he has worked all his life is a great thing."

Whatever the ultimate limitations of the plot, he portrayed the world of the shipyard worker with realism and wit. This was evident in a public house discussion of the hard times on the job front:

> DOYLE: What's the use of standing at the gate? Ye'd never get a start that way. Ye might have before the war, but they don't start hands that way now.
> HAGAN: That's true enough. Ye mind afore the war ye stood outside the boiler ship, or engine shop, and waited till the gaffer come out to start hands. Every man had as good a chance as another ... that was before the war. But now ... not the same at all. Ye've got to ambush him in some lonely part of the yard, to waylay him coming to his work

or on his road home ... ye've got to know his mother-in-law, or his wife's sister's cousin or some other near relation to speak for ye ... Bah, ye've got to act the oul' lady to get a man's job ... It's a damn shame, so it is! It doesn't give a fellow a chance that, looking work. In fact it means this, the less ye look the better chance ye have of getting a job.

It is doubtful if Doyle and Hagan's 'golden age' of recruitment practices in the shipyards ever existed, but the exchange makes evident how, by the 1920s, they enjoyed little more security than that of the casual docker dealing with the tyranny of the stevedore.

Carnduff's caustic wit is even more evident as the pair discuss the marital row at the centre of the play:

HAGAN: Why doesn't she divorce him?
BRADSHAW [*disgustedly*]: Do ye never think at all? Sure ye might know ye can't divorce anybody in Ulster!
HAGAN: They do it across the channel.
BRADSHAW: But we're not across the channel.
HAGAN: Ain't we part of the United Kingdom?
BRADSHAW: Aye, of course, but we're not a married part.

The repartee, humorous in itself, enables Carnduff to point up a narrow-mindedness on moral issues which he certainly opposed and, at the same time, to provide a splendid metaphor for what he viewed as the ambiguous relationship between Ulster and the United Kingdom.

It was not enough for the communist Mary Donnelly writing in *Workers Voice* who found the play suffering from "a final collapse to capitalist convention", while still hoping for "big things in the future from the pen of Comrade Carnduff".

Carnduff's next play, *Machinery*, again with a title redolent of proletarian drama, was performed by the Ulster Repertory Theatre in 1933, again travelling via the Abbey to the Empire. In the first act, the hero, Jack Power, a conscientious and self improving workman in the Samuel Smiles tradition, turns rebel when his wife is dragged into a machine and killed. Yet, by the last act, all conflict is resolved as it turns out that the boss, Norman Miller, is in fact a benevolent one:

POWER [*sincerely*]: Mr. Miller, ye have always been decent with me—no employer could have given a workman better chances of getting on than you have given me—but I hate machinery, sir—I'd just hate tae go back tae it.

But Miller is persuasive:

MILLER: But, my lad, you were destined to be an engineer whether you chose it or not—we may get set-backs—be turned in our tracks occasionally—but it is inevitable that we come back in to the same groove again—we can't help ourselves.

And with the encouragement of the rest of the workforce, Power returns to solve the mill's mechanical problems, and, incidentally, to find a new wife.

While this extract does not do justice to the effective dialogue between workers who suspect new machinery, to the banter of the factory floor, to powerful women dealing with drunken and violent husbands, the climax of the play clearly owes more to the Protestant work ethic and theories of predestination, than to any exploration of class conflict.

Carnduff could no longer rely so fully on his notoriety as the unemployed playwright. Thus Gerald O'Brien, writing in *The Ulsterman*, asked the serious question "What is Carnduff's position in the Irish theatre?" and went on to offer judgement:

He has been called the Sean O'Casey of the north. If that is taken to mean that he is the nearest thing we have to an O'Casey, it may be true. It should not mean anything more than that. O'Casey and Carnduff both grip us by the throat, but Carnduff lets us go just when we are beginning to enjoy the experience.

In 1934, Carnduff returned with an even more controversial theme in *Traitors*, which was set against the background of the unemployment crisis and the consequent riots in 1932. None of the text has been found, but at least one contemporary review gives a detailed summary:

Tom Russell, an unemployed joiner makes furniture at home while drawing the money from the buroo. Through the anonymous letter of a neighbour, he is found out. A Ministry of Labour clerk comes down on him at the actual moment his wife is dying.

Once again an unlikely resolution of conflict is at hand for although

"Russell is an embittered man following his wife's death and his own jail sentence ... the friendship of the official who has brought about his conviction secures him a job on his release". In real life, this could have been an echo of the support Carnduff had received from Richard Rowley, who in his non-literary persona, as G. V. Williams, was a Poor Law Guardian. In any case, the play did not in the end have a happy ending, as "tragedy follows on the evening before he [Russell] is to go back to work when he comes to his death in a riot at a proclaimed unemployment meeting".

As with his previous plays, critics like Gertrude Gaffney found "an untidy, badly constructed play", but, nonetheless, one "that holds one ... through the amount of good material, and good characterisation it contains", and yet it was to be the last contemporary social play by Carnduff to be given a professional stage performance.

Curiously, the autobiography casts no light on the unemployment riots of 1932 in which the fictional Russell of *Traitors* met his fate. We need not doubt Carnduff's sympathy with the cause of the Outdoor Relief men because, elsewhere, in his 'Odyssey of an Out-of-Work in the 1930s', he wrote:

> When the ODR men went on strike against their bitter position a wave of sympathy spread through the city on their behalf. Employers and traders were lavish in their gifts to assist them in their helplessness in the struggle. Food and monetary assistance poured into their common fund, making it possible to press their grievances against the cruel standards they were forced to live under.

Even this account lacks detail and any direct sense of involvement. Nor does Carnduff offer any enlightenment on the switch in mood in working-class areas which led to the riots of 1935. True, the autobiography does refer to these disturbances, but it does so in a curiously perfunctory way—the intimidation at work of a son who promptly joins the official Orange Order; the use of peace lines for the first time; and the problems that arose when Clifton Street Orange Hall was trapped on the wrong side of the lines.

Yet, as Noel Carnduff recalls, Hanover Street and the Old Lodge Road area were very much caught up in the trouble. At the top of Hanover Street was Trinity Street "a Catholic street and we were always warned not to go into that district". When the riots came "there were snipers from the top of the street shooting down the street". He recalls one particularly harrowing incident:

> One of my friends who lived opposite was from a mixed marriage ...

The family must have had a warning. They just vacated. They just went missing, and this so-called friend of the elder brother. I actually myself saw him go over with the key, opening the door and bringing all the furniture out to burn it ... That incident was such a betrayal.

It may have been that Thomas Carnduff saw sectarian violence as part of the normal course of city life, to be deplored, yes; to be opposed to in one's personal life, to be blamed on 'hot heads', but not especially noteworthy in itself.

Certainly as a journalist, and on occasion writing as 'Carndhu' in the Catholic *Irish News*, his outlook was poles apart from conventional loyalist rhetoric. Fairly fundamentally, he now questioned the advantages of partition:

> In pre-war days the ambition of every citizen was to see their native city develop into the first city in Ireland. Dublin had to be outclassed both in industry and population. Ten more years in a united Ireland and their ambition might have been realised. They preferred partition and so lost the benefit of competition. The loss of national and even provincial pride which followed the separation of the north from the rest of Ireland has not only lowered the political status of Belfast, but has also raised a barrier against the interchange of trade and commodities which has fallen heavily on many northern industries. No Belfastman can be foolish enough to admit that the city has prospered under partition.

He had revelled in the visits to Dublin with his plays and had made new friends, including Peadar O'Donnell, at this time involved in the Republican Congress Movement. He signed Carnduff's autograph book in 1934 and, perhaps, it was at this time that Carnduff presented him with an Independent Orange Order sash.

In contrast to unionist scorn for and hostility to the Catholic Eucharistic Congress of 1932, Carnduff argued that many Belfast traders were hoping that visitors to the Dublin celebrations would visit the north, and that many northerners would be interested in going to Dublin to see the associated celebrations.

In the meantime, a new direction in his dramatic interests promised a further journey along the knife edge of Ulster prejudices. Ruddick Millar, writing in the *Irish News* of 6th December 1934, announced Carnduff's "first incursion into costume drama" with a play dealing with "Lord Castlereagh and the '98 period". Millar concluded that "having read it for myself, I believe that the production will create something of a dramatic sensation". It was not, of course, an entirely new field of interest for Carnduff—he had, after all, lectured sympathetically on the men of '98 as far back as the 1920s. Nonetheless, just as he had stretched the limited conventions of the Belfast stage simply by portraying working men, so now *Castlereagh* was bound to be controversial by its very subject matter—no other local play of the inter-war years dared treat of such a sensitive theme in Ulster history.

Castlereagh opened at the Empire on 21st January 1935 and Carnduff was fortunate in his cast with Richard Hayward in the title role, Harold Goldblatt as Alexander Knox and R.H. McCandless as Jemmy Hope. It was immediately evident that Carnduff's talent for dialogue had transferred well to historical drama. Though some of his realisation of big house life was clumsy, the central confrontation—that between Hope and Castlereagh, was powerfully achieved:

> HOPE: Your lordship has not laboured in the fields for a mere pittance, nor been harnessed to a loom like a beast of burden. We were driven like brutes to our labour, and as we return to our brood—what would you have us do?
> CASTLEREAGH [*a far away look in his eyes*]: We could build a great Kingdom out of these islands, an Empire that would rule the world— No nation in Europe, no race on the face of the earth would dare question its power.
> HOPE: The people's power.

Note here that Hope is portrayed as driven to revolt, and the coherent ideological idealism is left to Castlereagh. Nor does Hope resist Castlereagh's dream of a great empire of the future, though he makes the distinction that, if created, it will be by 'people's power', not by Castlereagh's aristocratic power. This was not then a simplistic republican play. It was rather quite within the populist independent tradition of the 'masses' versus the 'classes', still seen as viable within an idealised concept of empire.

Much of the strength of the play lies in Carnduff's own ambivalence towards the protagonists, both of whom he evidently felt for. Indeed, Castlereagh is given the last powerful speech.

> CASTLEREAGH: Men are saying out there that I work for the bondage of our country—I who have striven night and day that it

might prosper and grow in importance—they do not understand ... Look! There stand the hills of Mourne—and there the wooded hills of Down—and, see—beyond the cluster of woodland—beautiful Strangford, with its water shining like a flawless mirror. [*with emotion*] God, how could any man betray such a land! [*Loudly in defiance*] They lie when they say I do not love my country, they lie, I tell you!

Sam Hanna Bell recalled that this was a declaration "which we in the Gods received in silence broken by a storm of jeers, groans and orange peel". Carnduff's description of the Chief Secretary as 'Bloody Castlereagh' was "cordially accepted by a large part of the audience", and Bell concludes that "the playwright made little effort to dissemble his sympathies".

This was a view taken by H. Montgomery Hyde, the unionist author of *The Rise of Castlereagh*, who attacked Carnduff on the grounds of historical inaccuracy—there was no evidence that Hope and Castlereagh had ever met—and on the grounds of undue sympathy for republican heroes. Carnduff replied arguing that "a dramatist does not write history; he makes use of it for the purpose of revealing the characteristics of the subject he wishes to portray". He turned the tables on Hyde by noting that "I found history and biography rather given to partisanship", and described his methods using "the better plan of studying the spoken or written words of my various characters".

While he was not advocating neutrality, his commitment to the contending characters of the play was more complex than either Hyde or Bell, from their differing perspectives, allowed. He admired Castlereagh for his "one ambition in life—to unite this country with Great Britain", and could not deny that "he served the State with a loyalty that has never been questioned", but in doing so "he served his class rather more than his country". By contrast, Carnduff held that the true definition of a patriot was "one who suffers in service, poverty or death being his only reward". He went on—"the leaders of the United Irishmen, with few exceptions suffered death. If I have been unduly sympathetic in portraying the rebel characters in my play, it is because of this".

The success of *Castlereagh* encouraged Carnduff to pursue the historical vein. The *Irish News* of 3rd April 1936 described how Carnduff was "working on a historical drama built around the siege of Derry in 1689". Carnduff went on to describe how he had "spent a day in Derry City last week touring the walls and surrounding countryside for atmosphere, as well as inspecting the old manuscripts preserved in the Protestant Cathedral for material". Apparently work was well advanced, sufficiently so for the reporter, Ruddick Millar, to describe how "Colonel Murray the defender of Derry, General Sarsfield, the Irish leader, King James II, Marshall Rosen, the French commander, and even Lundy are brought to life by Carnduff in his new play on one of Ulster's stirring epochs".

A short script, *The First Warrant*, dealing with the founding of the Orange Order after the battle of the Diamond, suggests that, while anxious to dramatise the key moments in Protestant working-class history, Carnduff was certainly not intent on providing Orangeism with a simple and propagandist mythology. He had already written the history in this conventional mould in 'The Battle at the Diamond', published in the *Orange and Purple Courier*. In this account, possibly provided for an Independent Orange readership, all that had delayed James Sloan in drawing up the first warrant was lack of a pen. Now, in Carnduff's dramatised account, matters were very different.

Here the Orange leader, Wilson finds James Sloan less than enthusiastic:

SLOAN: You yourself would admit that there are men in your ranks who would plunder and destroy in the holy name of religion and civil liberty without a thought of the ill will they were doing their neighbours.

Archdall, the local magistrate and landlord, is hostile to both—"What is the country coming to when the rabble take upon themselves the authority to grant commissions" and goes on to advocate the abolition of the Irish parliament and a new Act of Union "better for us all". Wilson, the Orangeman, retorts fiercely.

By all ye mean the nobility and gentry, not those who till the soil or ply the loom. It'll be an ill day when the country relinquishes its parliament to become servile to the English nation. God forbid that such a calamity should ever take place ... Is it not sufficient that you and your like should exploit us without handing us over to another country to add to our problems.

Sloan eventually provides the warrant, but for opportunistic reasons— "now there will be no reason for the military to billet on us"—and hopes that this will bring peace, and yet the play ends with the renewed sound of sectarian battle off stage.

In this play, Carnduff emphasised—even idealised—the democratic and popular base of Orangeism and its spirit of independence and even anti-Englishness; he portrayed the upper orders as either opportunistic in their use of Orangeism or downright hostile to its democratic tendencies, and yet, at the same time, he did not evade the negative face of popular Orangeism—its potential for involvement in sectarian conflict.

It would be wrong to suggest that all Carnduff's writing had an overt politico-cultural purpose. A full-length play *Jonathan Swift*, and a partly similar text, *The Young Jonathan Swift*, neither of which step on such tendentious ground, both date from roughly this period.

All these later historical works have it in common that they were never performed, or, in the case of *Derry*, have vanished without trace. It was in April 1936 that Carnduff had so confidently heralded this venture, and yet a month later, in the *Irish News*, he was giving voice to a new pessimism:

> A working man who cultivates a taste for literature and drama in Belfast has about as much chance of recognition as a sparrow has in the peacock enclosure at Bellevue.

Now he was scathing about the Ulster theatre:

> Deviation from the old established ideas of Ulster drama brings down wrath on the poor author who dares it, from those who have made Ulster drama what it is. Hugh Quinn tried it. His play travelled Dublin, London and Wales before it reached Belfast. Jack Loudan, Ruddick Millar, Harry Gibson broke fresh and difficult ground with their several plays. What encouragement did they get to repeat their initial efforts?

The Derry project had become a final challenge:

> With the completion of the historical play built around the Siege of Derry which I am working on at the moment, let it be successful or otherwise, I say to drama—never again!

And yet there is no evidence that it was completed, at least at this time. Carnduff's acquaintance with Denis Johnston may have encouraged the latter with his celebrated BBC documentary 'Lilibulero', but no more than that because, as we shall see, Carnduff was still struggling with his own *Derry* in the early '40s.

He himself was to identify a crisis of confidence and loss of momentum. Writing in September 1941, he described how "six years ago I had my hand at the top most rung of the ladder of success ... when something caused me to slacken and slow down. What it was is of no moment now". Here he seems to refer to some unrevealed crisis, yet the hostility of the environment in which he sought to progress must have played its part.

Disappointment with, or failure to complete, the Derry play, did not after all snuff out his urge to explore dramatically the possibilities of the 'independent' tradition. His next venture in this direction was a futuristic one, in *The Stars Foretell*, completed in 1938. It had been foreshadowed in a vein of journalistic writing, first in the *Irish News*, in 1935, when, as 'Sandy Row', he had written 'A Vision of the Future' predicting the defeat of the Unionists by a coalition of Independents and other opposition parties. Closer still to the plot of *The Stars Foretell* was 'Ireland's Future Parliament', written a year later for the *Sunday Independent*. This piece was sub-titled 'Merging of Green and Khaki Clad Soldiers: United Deputies sing the National Anthem', and here the Unionist Party was part of the government coalition within a united Irish parliament.

In *The Stars Foretell*, set in 1958, the unionists have indeed been defeated by the Independents and the new Independent Prime Minister, Mr. Graham, invited to Dublin on a courtesy visit, comes with his 'Ulster Territorials'. They are characterised very much as pre-First World War Young Citizen Volunteers, and seize control of the city, as part of an elaborate and bloodless stratagem to secure dominion status for Northern Ireland from an unwilling British government.

The play is of course satirical, and entirely subversive of the conventional unionist portrayal of the Protestant position in Ireland as a beleaguered one; doubly so because its writing coincided with de Valera's new constitution. Carnduff celebrates a Protestant competence and efficiency, quite capable of playing on an all-Ireland stage. In the political and sectarian climate of the late 1930s, the argument of *The Stars Foretell* was at least dangerously equivocal and it achieved no more than a reading to the members of the Young Ulster Society.

Despite the failure to achieve public performance of new ventures, *Castlereagh* enjoyed an amateur revival in 1939, but now there were other critics in the wings from his very own Independent Orange Order:

Dear Sir or Brother, I was instructed by the members and officers of Number 1 District Lodge to request you to attend Number 1 District meeting on Thursday 21st December at 8 pm A report appeared in the local press stating that you were present on a Sunday Evening in St. Peter's Roman Catholic Hall when a performance was given. If the report is true the District would like you to attend to give an explanation.

Fraternally Yours,
W. J. Moore
District Secretary

Thus, while much of Carnduff's enterprise in the 1930s had been devoted to developing a positive independent tradition, it appears that the real Independents, at least from 1935 onwards, had been retreating into the safe confines of traditional loyalism.

Whatever about their doubts, Carnduff still remained an acceptable representative of the working class in one other important and deeply conventional arena, that of the BBC. His collaboration with Denis Johnston, in December 1937, on 'Birth of a Giant', was one of the documentary landmarks of the decade—"a most realistic reconstruction of the building of a liner in the Belfast shipyard. Many of the scenes were remarkably well done, particularly as the men were being paid off at the launching ceremony". The scenario was clearly Carnduff's and, yet, in Rex Cathcart's history of the BBC in Northern Ireland, *The Most Contrary Region* (1984), Carnduff's role is air-brushed out. Carnduff succeeded in his own right with the play, *Industry*, broadcast in December 1939, but it was an isolated opportunity. True, he broadcast on 'A Dustman's Life' in July 1936, but essentially he was not called upon in any role other than that of working man.

Thus he had to turn to Radio Éireann for a performance of a conventional melodrama, *Murder at the New Road*, in 1937. The rapid shift of venue was noted by a reviewer who praised the play as "first class entertainment" but went on to remark, "it was originally, I believe, called *Murder at Stranmillis*" and, in spite of the southern brogue, it was possible to recognise the Lagan Enbankment as the scene of the crime". The reviewer then asked "I cannot understand why it was not broadcast from Belfast".

Carnduff was bitterly critical of the BBC. Writing in the *Irish News*, in May 1936, he commented:

> I had hopes of a revival in Ulster drama when ... the BBC entered the dramatic field. But they look with disfavour on historical drama with an Ulster setting, if it even skirts a political or religious background

... The past history of Ulster seems to be a closed book to our station directors. Yet we have to listen to the Duke of Monmouth's rebellion, or the '45 Rising, or some historical episode depicting English or Scottish history.

If they did not value him for anything else, Carnduff was essential to the BBC when they wanted to popularise the first wartime Christmas broadcast to the Empire in December 1939. Who better to provide an authentic script for working people all pulling together on the Home Front than him?

MRS. GRAY: More Pudding, Lily?
LILY: No thanks, Mrs. Gray.
MRS. GRAY: What about you, Johnny?
JOHNNY: I couldn't, ma.

It was hardly the stuff of controversy, yet an extraordinary row about 'vulgar' speech followed. An investigative reporter from the *Belfast Telegraph* tracked the Gray's to their Denmark Street home and scene of the outside broadcast, because "wires were still connected". Here Mrs. Gray "hastened to say that in their every day conversation the words 'Ma' and 'Da' were never used, their son and daughter having been taught to refer to their parents as 'Mummy' and 'Daddy'" Mr. Gray then explained "that the script had been written by Mr. Carnduff".

Carnduff was well able to defend himself in the face of this astonishing witch hunt and wrote to the *Telegraph*:

The Gray family could not hide their Belfast accent, no more than I, even if they tried; and my own is particularly piercing. Why should I be ashamed of it? I was born in Belfast. It was certainly a big honour for Jimmy Gray and his family to be chosen as representatives of an Ulster family life in an Empire Broadcast, but it wasn't all the honour—the microphone was honoured to have such a family facing it.

Facing the pressures of social snobbery, in addition to the travails of a city still ensnared in sectarian suspicion, and with a theatre at best faltering and cautious, Carnduff still found time to create yet another area of space in which he could operate. He did this by building on ambitions first expressed in the 1920s through the Poetry Society and the Independent Literary and Debating Society:

The idea had taken root in the mind of a certain old veteran that Belfast, and the north in general, had fallen behind Dublin in cultural activities, and why not gather a number of young people together to put enthusiasm into a movement which might encourage a new interest in all forms of art in Ulster.

The "old veteran" was, of course, Carnduff, and, in November 1936, the Young Ulster Society was duly launched at a public meeting in the YMCA addressed by Denis Ireland, Richard Hayward and Major Jack Henderson. In the next few years, it was to host many of the more significant cultural figures of the period including Lynn Doyle, Oliver St. John Gogarty, Denis Ireland, Denis Johnson, Michael MacLaverty and Peadar O'Donnell and, by March 1940, it could count 140 members.

Carnduff's previous emphasis on working-class involvement in such affairs was less to the fore. By the outbreak of the war, the Society could boast membership "from practically every profession and trade in the city ... Among our members we have a clergyman and a doctor, a novelist and biographer, an artist, quite a number of playwrights and poets, journalists, critics and teachers, as well as bank clerks, typists" and only then "artisans". Then there were also Queens University "graduates and undergraduates".

In the first issue of *Young Ulster*, published in October 1938, Carnduff had to admit—"we have not accomplished a great amount of progress", that is in the society's mission to "encourage a greater knowledge of Ulster art, literature, and drama." This was a failure reflected in the thin content of this and the following two issues of *Young Ulster*, despite the popularity of the society.

In the second issue K.H. Giddens while acknowledging "the gay and sometimes distinguished Tuesday night throng in the Lombard [Café]" suggested that "our meetings have become the monopoly of two types of person: the gifted and confident, and the escapists who bask in the reflected glory of the great". At the end of the day, Giddens found "a lack of adventure [and] a one-sided exhibition of knowledge".

While the criticism may have had some validity, the Young Ulster Society remained the only significant forum for cultural discussion in Belfast well into the 1950s.

The society did provide a platform for Carnduff's own critique of the state of Ulster culture, and for his not always consistent solutions. Thus, in October 1938, he argued that "we must remember that our literature, poetry and drama are Irish and should remain Irish. The moment we remove our provincial dialect from our Literature and drama we will develop into a second-rate English county".

He found the "Six Counties ... isolated from political contact with the south, and deprived of the educational value of the Irish academical institutions", and yet a six counties which "still stand aloof from English thought and literature, grimly clinging to their traditional speech and customs".

In theatre, he argued that the Abbey and Gate in Dublin needed "to broaden their repertoire to include the native speech of the north. The alternative is, of course, a 'National' theatre for Ulster in Belfast", one in which he saw risks—"the danger of the two 'national' theatres is the probable development of two national outlooks".

More generally, he argued that "there is no province, county or city boundary within which can be set up a claim to a monopoly of Ireland's culture; and Ireland owes too much to Ulstermen for their part in building Irish civilisation to allow even six of her counties to be pushed aside".

Thus Carnduff mirrored some of the arguments of the founders of the Ulster Literary Theatre before the First World War. Now, in 1938, he could certainly be read as a cultural Irish nationalist, and yet by the third issue of *Young Ulster* published sometime after the outbreak of the Second World War, he was arguing that "it should be the ultimate aim of all lovers of drama in the north to establish in Belfast a national theatre for Ulster".

The year 1939 marked a watershed in Carnduff's life and not merely because of the outbreak of war. In the early part of the year, his first wife Susan died after a short illness at the relatively early age of 51, "worn out by the cares of life". Writing to a friend, Theresa Lee, in June, he referred to "the slice of trouble which I hope I have got over now" and went on to describe how he had managed a week's holiday in Dublin.

> Spent the most brilliant holiday of my life there. I met a host of friends ... Maurice Walsh, Longford, R.M. Fox. I spent a weekend opposite de Valera's house in Booterstown, but I didn't see him to my regret. I was up at Bulmer Hobson's house too. I wasn't very comfortable there. I don't think he has half the vitality he had in the old days.

The attractions of Dublin remained, but he was soon facing the harsh realities of home life in the absence of a wife—"I never thought there was so much trouble keeping a home going till now", and then there was the outbreak of war which he initially viewed as "a blooming nuisance." He was immediately transferred to ARP duty and suffered "complete sleeplessness" but, happily for him, his lack of enthusiasm was matched by that of the authorities who called off the fire-watching "because of expense and I wasn't sorry".

It is in this war period that we know most of the personal Carnduff because he fell in love with Mary McElroy and married her in 1941, and his extensive correspondence to her, commencing in 1940 but mainly covering late 1942 and 1943, survives. Unlike many another wartime separation of lovers, this one was forced on Carnduff and his second wife because they faced family difficulties in making the relationship known, as was evident from Carnduff's letter of proposal:

> Richard Rowley would be one of the witnesses, you choose the other. When we would take up house together would be for you to decide. Where we would live I leave up to you. How or when we would break the news to your family or friends would be with you. If you would rather I kidnap you pass the word. If you want me to come down to Cloneen and cause a riot just let me know.

In the event, they were married secretly but, for at least two years, the connection remained a covert one. She lived in Greenisland, he remained in Belfast. Fleeting meetings were supplemented by the constant flow of letters which, even if devoted to love, could not evade the impact of war. The Blitz found Carnduff "scared, scared just about as stiff as any man can be", and left Hanover Street badly damaged, and as he moved out Carnduff realised that an era was over and not necessarily for the worse:

> Tomorrow No. 7 passes into oblivion. Everything in the house is going to be destroyed except for a few pieces of furniture which I prize. The house has memories which are not always pleasant to dwell on, sometimes horrifying, occasionally astounding, when I think what I accomplished in such surroundings under conditions when most men would smother with despair and downright sickness.

As a prolific correspondent, Carnduff could not resist the documentary role and, in October 1942, suggested that his letters would constitute "a journal to Mary ... which would mean a letter to you every day describing what people are doing, saying, thinking, during these extraordinary times". Although the daily ambition was not fulfilled, they provide a vivid record of the following two years.

He remained cynical about many aspects of the war effort and, while lambasting those in power, questioned the commitment of the ordinary man in the street. As to his own civil defence work, the first comment came on All Hallows' Eve 1942, when he recorded the squalid drunkenness of his colleagues, and a month later he gave a more overall perspective:

> This is the laziest job I have ever been up against. My opinion regarding the personnel of Civil Defence isn't very high. There's always a grouse if they are asked to do too much. Yet they volunteer to go out on farm work willingly. But then we pay them and so do the farmers. In other words they get two day's pay for one day's work. Talk about a national conscience.

He was even less persuaded by pomp and ceremony—as he made clear in an account of Civil Defence Day on Sunday 21 November 1942:

> There were services in all the largest halls. Members of the Civil Defence paraded in force, 5,000 of them, I think ... All the 'Big Nobs' were at the saluting base as the Services marched past. These uniform parades always give me a sore head. Most of those who 'took the Salute' also took to their heels during the Belfast blitzes.

That same autumn he offered only the most grudging welcome to the arriving American troops:

> I don't think the authorities give a damn what Ulster people had to say about this friendly invasion. They were dumped here and that was all about it. I wish you could see their tanks, lorries and cars which crowd the Lagan boulevards. They have about a mile and a half of the embankment closed off to the public with armed sentries at either end. Of course we may need them all before this war comes to an end. Two of their soldiers received ten years imprisonment last week for beating a publican to death with their tin helmets.

He noted one immediate consequence, the appearance of notices in lavatories warning of the dangers of venereal disease—"the first time in living memory that the corporation have worried about this terrible scourge. Up till now they've suffered from bashfulness."

Nor, as the war went on, did he see much general increase in patriotic fervour. Commenting, in March 1943, he singled out "merchants and businessmen [who] wax fat on war", but went on to observe that "munitions workers rarely look on their labour as a patriotic gesture" and that "the majority of people these days seem to think war a good investment and are not worrying very much whether it continues a few more years".

It was a climate fit for cutting humour. In the same letter, he reported that "an outstanding event occurred here yesterday. A young Belfast man joined the army. It caused a sensation in his district. Nobody could understand what had happened to cause such a tragedy". A month later, he commented in similar vein that "if one gathers a fair amount of salvage, old tins, waste paper and such like one is making a suitable effort to win decorations in Belfast".

Nor did war mean an end to political and sectarian tensions, as was evident in the Lower Falls area where Carnduff was posted in late 1942. The area was still affected by the ongoing IRA campaign and, in October, he noted that "Albert Street district is still under curfew, although there hasn't been any shooting lately. The police seem to have the IRA gunfighters well in hand. I haven't much trouble in getting to my ARP post at night, yet I retain the habit of hugging the cover of buildings just in case a bomb might go off".

In November, he was irritated that "these Catholic mates of mine at the Post keep tuning in to hear Lord Haw-Haw". Although he commented tolerantly that "I believe they are more anti-British than pro-German", the old loyalist twitch re-surfaced in the comment "If I had another Protestant companion to back me up I'd put an end to the Lord Haw-Haw broadcast in a Civil Defence Post".

In one area, Carnduff reflected unionist fears of war-time change, objecting to the "retaining subsidy" paid to key workers from Éire, and worrying about the implications of emigration from Ulster to war work in Britain, and the prospect of a consequent change in the religious balance of the population.

Curiously, Carnduff's most direct experience of anti-IRA measures came when they affected friends of his. In December 1942, members of the Young Ulster Society were amongst those who had their houses raided, and Denis Ireland's Unity Club, which shared overlapping membership, was more directly affected:

Ford Graham, one of our little circle who have coffee every morning in Campbell's Cafe has been detained in prison under the Civil Powers Act. He is a member of Denis Ireland's Unity Club, and is an advocate of Republicanism, still I like him. He is being dismissed from a comfortable position in an insurance company. All this because his younger brother [John Graham], a member of the IRA deservedly received a sentence of 12 years penal servitude for firing on the police.

While Carnduff's hostility to the IRA campaign was straightforward, he objected to guilt by association:

> The Grahams are Protestants. If Ford Graham had been a Catholic, his brother's crime would have been accepted as a matter of fact and he himself would probably have been allowed to hold whatever opinions he liked. Ford's life was spent in the Protestant community and so he became ostracised from the rest of the people. His being persecuted because of his brother's crime is accepted as being just retribution.

In this assessment, Carnduff was certainly painting an altogether too rosy picture of the fate of Catholic families tainted by arrests, but was undoubtedly commenting perceptively on the difficulties of Protestant radicals. While Ford Graham was a Republican, Carnduff may have had in mind too the potential for ostracisation even of those who, like himself, merely played devil's advocate, and stepped from the narrow confines of cultural unionism.

For him, some aspects of traditional faith remained unchanged. He chided Mary in October 1942 that they had spent the day together when "we should have been attending some place of worship". The following month, when they missed a meeting, he "travelled down to Dunmurry church and listened to an extraordinarily fine sermon [and] the discussion group which met after the service settled post-war reconstruction inside an hour and a half".

Yet if a basic faith flourished, a long standing anti-clericalism remained equally in the ascendant. In November 1942, he derided the Rev. Barron of Whitehouse who had died leaving £14,000 to build a new church at Glengormley—"one could hardly visualise the entire population [of Whitehouse] possessing 14,000 coppers, let alone pounds. Some clergymen are supermen." A month later, he was gleefully reporting the prosecution of another prominent Presbyterian minister, the Reverend Wylie Blue, for "contravention of the petrol restrictions".

His estrangement from the Independent Orange Order, which was apparent over the *Castlereagh* incident in 1939, was not mended in wartime. Indeed, three letters in November 1942 suggest a more general questioning of the relevance, or even rightness, of Orangeism. He had come to the conclusion that "flag waving and drum beating are now a thing of the past". On 21 November, he recorded as a matter of note that "The Grand Orange Lodge held a meeting here last week". It was a matter of note because "I haven't heard of anyone attending an Orange Lodge meeting these last two years. All the banner painters have gone out of business. Most of the lodges have gone out of business too". More fundamental was his conclusion that this was "all for the good of the city".

A week later and he was writing in satirical vein:

> I was passing an Orange Hall last Sunday and noticed half a dozen show posters lined across the front entrance ... "Amazing Bible Fulfilment explained, on Sunday at 11 am" Beside this was another;—"Tap Dancing Tuition on Tuesdays and Thursdays." A coloured poster announced "Dance to Jim Patterson's Band every Monday and Saturday." Another;—"The Apostolic Church meets here for Prayer at 7 pm Sundays." To crown it all the Independent Orangemen themselves announced;—"A Gospel meeting every Sunday at 3 pm, under the auspices of the Orange institution." Three years ago dancing was tabooed from the hall by the Orangemen themselves. War can change even religious prejudices.

In such desperate circumstances, the Independents had evidently buried the hatchet and their principles with the official order, the 'crown' to Carnduff's contempt.

It was more difficult to find an amenable political home beyond Independent Orangeism. Carnduff's war-time letters were certainly well-laced with a radical social critique, thus he denounced infant mortality rates in Belfast or, in December 1942, reflected on the economic failures of the inter-war years—"Look at the indictment of private enterprise and business management. Since 1918, 35 weaving factories, 18 spinning mills, and all the print works except two have closed down in Ulster".

Now, above all, one might have expected him to move closer to the Northern Ireland Labour Party, and yet his first comment in December

1942 on the split caused by Harry Midgley's resignation to form the Commonwealth Labour Party is remarkable for its uninvolved tone:

> Harry Midgley has split the Labour Party. Very few were surprised. There has always been a dividing line amongst the members. The Catholic members have always leaned towards the Republican ideal, the Protestants cleave naturally towards a closer union with the British Labour Party. Midgley challenged the issue and they expelled him. Now Midgley aspires to lead an imperialistic Labour group in Ulster. I think Labour on the whole will suffer. They were never too strong in Belfast.

Carnduff, for all his cynicism, was now increasingly committed to the war effort, not least with sons now in the forces and one in a prisoner-of-war camp. In the context of the Midgley dispute, he sought to set down his own viewpoint:

> For myself, I regret I have to admit I am an imperialist. I want to see the allies win, especially the British Empire. I too am to blame, as much as anybody, for prolonging the struggle, yet, in my heart, I believe there will be an opportunity after the war for men and women to assist with their own individual strength in re-organising the nations of the world under a new system that would bring peace and happiness to mankind.

He certainly brushed off overtures, in February 1943, from the Labour Party:

> Those Labour people were after me again to help them visualise their aspirations. I can visualise OK but not much more. They've grand rooms nearby, whist drives, rambles, debates, reading circles; they're very much alive but I don't like politics. I told them so. They say its not politics they want me for but cultural activities—sez they!

This despite the crisis of confidence in the Unionist government evident by April 1943 when he commented: "There is great dissatisfaction with the Northern government. It is held in contempt by every person. We haven't a solitary politician in the cabinet who holds the confidence of the people." At this point, he appears to have been more interested in the growth of the

Communist Party than the fortunes of either Labour or Midgley, noting that "it is considered quite fashionable to hold communistic opinions and unfashionable to hold patriotic demonstrations".

He was sufficiently moved to see the film, 'A Day of War in Russia', which was "a gruesome cycle of blood destruction and gallantry". Disappointed by the audience response, he was himself sympathetic—"I still can't tell whether the audience were stunned into silence or were merely bored. At the conclusion of the film there wasn't the slightest appreciation of the Russians and their heroism."

This brief interest ended with the communist popular front strategy— "Their latest move is that a coalition government should be formed out of all parties. They don't even mention their own possibilities. They're becoming quite conservative."

Elsewhere, he had never actually expressed sympathy for Midgley and, with the fall of the government in April 1943 and the formation of a new government including Midgley, another betrayal of the ordinary man was at hand:

> It looks probable that Harry Midgley will secure his reward for wrecking the Labour Party. It is rumoured that he becomes Labour minister in the new government. J.F. Gordon, the present minister, was also a socialist before he was offered the post. Isn't it funny dear, what a decent salary can do to make a man broad-minded.

Carnduff had perhaps finally escaped the embrace of politics, and yet other arenas of public life were increasingly wearying, certainly by comparison with the liveliness of his relationship with Mary. In June 1941, his very own creation, the Young Ulster Society, roused at least mock irritation by organising a hike over the Cave Hill—"Strange as it may seem, they propose following our route. Imagine the cheek of those people, and mind you, I had no say in it."

Disillusion had set in with a vengeance by October 1942:

> Women were in a preponderance of about eight to one. This often puzzles me at these literary meetings ... From my position, facing the audience, I can study their expressions. My dear, its very tiresome looking into tired dull faces. Most of these women are between the ages of thirty and forty. Probably they have side-tracked the fullness of life through fear or inability to grasp opportunities, and this is their

way of escape—to seek romance in words and illusions rather than face the ventures and pains of life in the full.

Disillusion had turned to desperation by March 1943—"If they would only go into hysterics, or throw the chairs about, or disagree with the lecturers, it would still bring some sort of action into the place." Carnduff's complaint about the literary life of the town was not confined to the Young Ulster Society. He was a founder of PEN and, in that capacity, attended a packed meeting in December 1942 addressed by Jan Masaryk, the Foreign Minister of the Czech government in exile. "Jan Masaryk, gave a fine speech" but "the place was crowded with third rate writers and a host of non-writers". The majority of the audience was "flowery frocked and uninteresting old ladies", and "The Chairman, a one time High Court Judge in India, sported a monocle, and the most pronounced Oxford accent. He almost roused the meeting to enthusiasm when he sat down".

As for himself, wartime did not initially curtail his writing plans. Soon after the outbreak of war he told Theresa Lee "I am trying to write a new play on the 1920 troubles with a political background" and, by March 1940, he was "just finishing *Curfew*", presumably the same play, and was planning "a private reading shortly". In April 1941, he was planning to give Richard Haywood till the end of the week to settle about *Curfew*, yet we hear no more of it. If it had surfaced, it would have served to illuminate, by theme at least, one of the blanks in the history of his own life. It would also have dealt with themes more controversial than those of any of his other plays, sufficiently so that it could hardly have been easily performed in Belfast, even with the arrival of the new Group Theatre. The following year he told Mary that he was "sketching out a Belfast/Dublin play showing a blitzed out Belfast family who go to Dublin and are killed along with their Dublin friends", but this project vanishes.

Many certainly encouraged him with the autobiography and also persuaded him to take up the *Derry* project once more. An undated letter, probably from mid-1941, suggests that this had got far behind:

> I was with the Group Theatre people last Friday and they're wobbly as to where they'll get the costumes from for *Derry*. I didn't argue when they suggested postponing the play, for one reason. Its production was to be my wedding present to you. Now, if the Abbey people suggest putting it on—and, Mary, pray that they do—I would cancel the Group production.

Was it *Derry* or *Curfew* or yet another project that he had in mind when he recounted a meeting with Bob McCandless, one of the directors of the Group Theatre, who was "keen on the play and thinks the rest favour it going on before the holidays", and yet nothing happened. It was becoming a pattern and, in truth, his career as a creative writer had almost run its course.

Certainly, he did not feel that the war-time atmosphere encouraged serious drama. Writing in November 1942 he noted that:

> The Group Theatre are doing *The Rival* this week. There's an English farce at the Opera House, a revue in the Empire, and some second class pictures in the cinemas. You can put on any kind of show just now and be certain to make a profit. The people merely crowd into places of amusement, aimlessly, and without any choice.

Only one surviving playscript, *Give Losers Leave to Talk* dates from after the war, and this opens effectively against the background of the post-war housing crisis, with the tension of the generations between father (Harry) and son (Jimmie) thrown in:

> HARRY: Why aren't ye satisfied with what ye have until something turns up.
> JIMMIE: That's the danger, Dad, being satisfied. I want a decent place to rear me family in.
> HARRY [*rising to his feet*]: Ye mean—this isn't a decent place.
> JIMMIE: Ye know right well I didn't mean it that way. A fella wants a home where he can rear his family in his own way. Where he can have a bath ...
> HARRY: Holy Heavens! Did I ever object to any of youse having a bath.
> JIMMIE: But there isn't a bath in the house, Dad.
> HARRY: What's wrong with yer mother's big tin bath.

There is no evidence that it was performed. From war end also, as he and Mary adopted a more settled life, their correspondence peters out. Occasional sallies, whether from the chair of the Young Ulster Society or in journalistic form still surfaced.

He saw little sign of a new cultural enlightenment brought about by the war-time experience. In theatre, it was argued that because the "public have had to face too much tragedy ... they need cheering up". Thus when the Group Theatre had available a talent like that of Joseph Tomelty, "the most promising playwright since George Shiels", his ability to "excel at light comedy" was encouraged, at the expense of his more serious promise as represented by *All Souls' Night*.

Brick-bats were offered in other directions too—to the BBC for "its present policy of qualifying only professors and university graduates to speak for the entire community on art, literature and the problems of everyday life".

Were these the cantankerous musings of one who was no longer an active participant in the creative scene? Other commentators, such as Sam Hanna Bell, have suggested at least a slow broadening in the cultural environment of the post-war years and with some truth. Yet Carnduff, as with his character, Jimmie, in *Give Losers Leave to Talk* quite justifiably had a perspective that "the danger" was in "being satisfied".

Following his retirement from work with the Corporation in or about 1951, he had a renewed opportunity to make himself heard. Fortunately, he secured the not particularly onerous job of caretaker of the Linen Hall Library. This came complete with accommodation and give him free rein to the collections of the city's most historic library.

The biography project was once again revived but along with it went a rash of newspaper articles. Criticism of the Ulster theatre continued unabated and he argued that "the Ulster drama movement has today degenerated to the lowest level yet reached in regional drama". He was no mere isolated maverick and won the support of Joe Tomelty who 'agreed' and announced his own plan to start a new theatre producing mainly Irish plays, a venture tragically cut short by Tomelty's devastating car accident in 1953. Even those he criticised now acknowledged his role—in 1954, Harold Goldblatt acknowledged that Carnduff had "done much towards starting the movement out of which the Group Theatre had sprung". Carnduff, in turn, lent his weight to the campaign for a proper home for the theatre in 'The Case for an Ulster State Theatre' which appeared in the *Northern Whig* in December 1955.

The continued complexity of Carnduff's broader cultural outlook was best reflected in contributions to *The Bell*, now under the editorship of his old friend Peadar O'Donnell. 'The Orange Society', which appeared in 1951, was a simple defence of the cause, lacking any critical element and ceasing to make much distinction between the Independent tradition and that of the official order. It is from about this time that we have photograph of Carnduff with his son Joe, both wearing orange sashes, on the roof of the

Linen Hall Library. Clearly he was not prepared to break the umbilical cord with his own community.

Yet chameleon-like, and depending on circumstance, his *alter ego* came into play. Speaking to James Kelly of the *Irish Independent*, he affirmed "I have always been a Presbyterian '98 man ... and my ancestors lie in Drumbo churchyard in the shadows of a round tower". Carnduff's own sympathy with the United Irishmen was established at an early stage, but here he affixes his ancestors not merely to the radicalism of the United Irishmen but to romantic Irish tradition. This although the autobiography gives those very same ancestors a staunch Orange and Tory lineage. Romantic nationalism was carried a step further when he claimed that "a year could see the whole edifice of the border crumble".

The difficulties of Carnduff's true position were perhaps most effectively explored in 'Belfast is an Irish City', which appeared in *The Bell* in 1952. Flattering his mainly Dublin-based audience, he confessed that "Dublin is in the minds of all of us who write books or plays; in a vague sort of way it is our capital city", and yet he went on to argue that:

> Many things happen which make us think that the South is not adult minded enough to accommodate people of our freedom of thought within a United Ireland. Perhaps if we were patriots we should be prepared to risk some hardship and unfairness and trust to the future for the remedy, but then we are not patriots. We are merely Irishmen.

Carnduff cited the saying of the rosary at Easter commemorations. It was not that he objected to the commemoration. It was not that he objected to the saying of the rosary in its proper place "at religious ceremonies", but he did object to it at "the public ceremony [which] should be open to all creeds or no creed".

Then again there was the language question. He conceded that "very few of us take much interest in Gaelic tradition" but, nonetheless, "we would be quite pleased to learn that those who are interested in the language are making headway. Many of us would even encourage our children or grandchildren to learn it, and we would gladly see them off to Donegal for a holiday among the Gaelic speakers". There is however a determined downside—"we would not wish that our children would have to acquire their education through Gaelic and we are afraid that might happen to them in a United Ireland".

While nationalists were guilty of a "lack of consciousness" in recognising the "minority problem" of the Protestants in Ireland, he was "not suggesting that the Protestants of Ireland have not been reactionaries on the main question of the day, political independence". While he looked askance at unpalatable features of the southern sate, he now, more than ever before, expressed "impatience with sectarian strife in Belfast" and analysed its consequences.

No doubt he spoke very much for himself when he described how "the mind is intimidated and confused by it, and worse than all it spreads a feeling that the people are powerless before it and cannot dominate their circumstances". As for the writer "the mischief does not end there. This intimidation of the mind enters every sphere of cultural life. The artist is shut in too. Writers who make their living in State or Municipal employment have to be ever on guard over what they write ... ". He concluded that "there is a cultural problem in Ireland deriving from a sectarian problem, and Irish writers are not as conscious as they should be. Is it that they do not see, or that they dodge it?"

He died in April 1956, and the Young Ulster Society organised an evening devoted to his memory, addressed by Dr. Agnew, Denis Ireland, Jack Loudan, Peadar O'Donnell and others. In that 1952 article in *The Bell* he had, in fact, written the most effective epitaph for his times. Times in which, as John Hewitt wrote, so many apparently creative spirits:

> Finding themselves in an extroverted, stubborn inarticulate society with well defined material values and, for the most part, a rigid creed, revolted against their condition, became "minority minded", perpetually and consistently in opposition, and lacking the capacity to last it out, fled ...
> —'The Bitter Gourd', *Lagan*, 1945

Carnduff was not amongst them. The mainspring of his energy came from that "stubborn inarticulate society" which was his own, and remained so. That did not preclude a perpetual tendency to 'revolt', though it did condition and limit the nature of its expression.

Re-examination of his writings, as in performance by the Tinderbox Theatre Company in March 1991, will, as Ian Hill suggested at the time, "show up both the strength and weakness of his work", with the poems now seen as overly dominated by "sentimentality and doggerel". By contrast, "both the autobiography and plays are stiffened with a withering irony ... and a finely tuned sense of outrage at the conditions of urban workers".

Ultimately his worth lies beyond any narrow literary judgement. Rather, it lies in his consistent determination to pursue an independent cultural course founded within a powerful Protestant working-class culture, which was, if anything, increasingly suspicious of any such venture. At the same time, the possibilities of his endeavour were constantly threatened by the suffocating social prejudices and snobbery of middle-class Ulster.

The fact that his is the sole surviving substantial testimony of its kind from the entire period is witness enough to the difficulty of what he attempted. Resurrection of his life now is timely, in conditions in which many of the dilemmas with which he grappled remain unresolved.

John Gray
26th April 1994

The Autobiography of Thomas Carnduff

Preface

Do you remember those little two up, two down houses, where the coal was kept underneath the stairs in the kitchen and the dust bin had to be carried from the back-yard, right through the house, once a week, for emptying? One of those streets was Hanover Street, squeezed between the Crumlin and Shankill Roads. If you could have seen into number seven you would have seen my father sitting at a cane card table, tapping at a portable typewriter, which was perched precariously on the table. My two elder brothers dolling themselves up, ready for a session at the College dance hall where they both gave lessons; my younger brother and myself playing round our father's feet and my mother busying herself with housework. How many authors could compose and type a play in those conditions?

Later, he rented a small office in Donegall Street. It had no heating so, in the winter, he often worked with his coat on and wearing woollen gloves.

He contributed to all the local papers with poems and articles, the proceeds helped us from sinking completely in the swamps of poverty where we were firmly stuck as he had been unemployed for four years. His first play, *Workers*, was staged at the old Empire Theatre and played to full houses, twice daily, for a week. His reward—£15. However, it threw us a life line out of the swamp.

He was born 30th January 1886, in a street off Sandy Row. His mother died while he was still very young, his father in 1900, so he was an orphan at fourteen, the youngest of five children. He spent four years at the Royal Hibernian Military School in Dublin while his father was serving in the Bengal Lancers in India, served in the Specials (February 1922-December 1925), joined the Young Citizen Volunteers (October 1912). He married my mother in 1909, they had two sons pre-war and my younger brother and myself post-war. Father served in the Royal Engineers and spent a long time in France during the war.

Apart from his poems and articles, he wrote and acted in one and two act plays at the York St. non-subscribing Presbyterian Church, where amateur dramatics were just one of the many interests that the Reverend Doctor Agnew fostered.

His play, *Workers*, was rejected by the Grand Opera House as being too controversial. Richard Hayward (director of the Belfast Repertory Company) then took it to the Empire in Belfast and the Abbey in Dublin. It was very well received by critics and audiences alike. It had one criticism, from a communist paper, which thought it was not radical enough.

People in Belfast, researching my father's works, have asked me if he was a member off the Labour Party. Yes, he was, but not an active one, though he attended their meetings in Frederick Street but that was because he gloried in debate, anywhere, any subject.

Though he was a member of the Labour Party he distrusted politicians. In a letter to Mary (my stepmother) he states: "Those Labour people were after me again, to help them visualise their aspirations. I can visualise OK but not much more. I don't like politics. I told them so. They say it is not politics they want me for but cultural activities. Sez they!"

In 1936, he founded the Young Ulster Society. Its aim was "to encourage all forms of art in Ulster". The society was a great success. At one time, it had over 200 members and had speakers from every branch of the arts and very lively debates. When he retired as Chairman, the members voted him Life President and presented him with a portrait they had commissioned William Conor to paint. He later presented it to the Ulster Museum. He was a founder member of the Northern Ireland PEN club.

He was in great demand as a lecturer. One story he often related was of a visit to Lurgan College for a lecture to the students. The headmaster invited him to his study for a meal. When he was offered the trifle dish to help himself from he immediately devoured the lot! On looking up he knew he had made a blunder. The headmaster passed it off as though it was an everyday occurrence and even invited him back the following year.

My mother had never taken any interest in father's literary life, she was too busy cleaning for and attempting to feed a husband and four growing sons on a shoe-string; an effort which, in the end, wore her out and resulted in her death in 1939. The certificate stated 'natural causes'. Thank Heavens those natural causes, so common in those days, are uncommon today.

Mary, on the other hand, shared his interests but by now, with the exception of Sammy (my youngest brother) we had all moved on: Jim, the eldest, married; Joe and myself were in the Navy. So, life was a lot easier for dad now. He was in the ARP as a telephonist cum caretaker at Park Lodge, a big house on the Antrim Road, at the foot of Belfast Castle, where volunteers were trained.

Mary edited his works, filed and generally looked after his works and manuscripts. We sons owed her a lot for the devotion and happiness she brought back into dad's life. He was that rarity, a man who shared his life with two of nature's ladies. He spent his last years as caretaker at the Linen

Hall Library. He was very happy there, living with a multitude of books, his third great love.

One of his best friends was the well-known Dublin writer Peadar O'Donnell, who was also a staff officer in the IRA. On one of his visits to Dublin, dad presented Peadar with his Orange sash. (He was Worshipful Grandmaster at the time.) Peadar had it on show at his home, enshrined in a glass case. Last year, the sash was returned to me as Peadar, seriously ill, had requested one of his friends to return it to the family.

During the interview on TV, last year, after opening an exhibition on his life at the Linen Hall Library which was timed to coincide with a radio programme titled 'Reds, Radicals and Reformers' (one of the series featured my father), I was questioned as to which I thought he was. My answer—Reformer, of course.

Although many people thought his plays were political, I think, except for *Castlereagh*, he just drew pictures, with words, of life in the two up, two down working-class houses of the time.

I would be biased to pass an opinion on the merits of my father's works. His character you can judge from the biography. All I can say is that, at the time, he was the odd-man-out, a working man who was a poet and playwright. He set a mould that others followed. He was a kind man who took life's knocks with a shrug, its gifts with appreciation. One of his greatest pleasures came from helping others, especially younger writers.

I think he was a great man who still made time to be a great father. I could not have chosen a better one.

After an absence of some thirty years, I returned to Belfast during 1986 to find that most of my father's writing was missing, apart from a copy of his last play, *Castlereagh*, and his two books of poems.

I was, as you can guess, very sad and disappointed. Since then, I have returned many times searching with, I might add, quite a bit of success.

I have found all his many articles, some unproduced plays but most frustrating was to find that the third act was missing from his play, *Machinery*.

The following pages contain all I can find of his autobiography. The early years are missing but I think it has a lot to interest the Irish public.

Noel Carnduff
30th May 1994

Chapter One

'No load for a young child'

I

The Boer War was at its height when I bade farewell to the Hibernian School and returned home for good. Meanwhile, my eldest sister and brother had married during my stay in Dublin. I have no recollection of the entire family living at home at anytime. There was always a member of the family absent. My brothers, sisters and I never had an opportunity of mixing in the usual family circle. There was never any particular affection displayed when we did meet. All my affection and youthful homage was centred around my father.

He occupied the enclosure reserved for mother, brother, and sister. He was my world. Physically, he was now a complete wreck. The resultant effects of his service in India had not only blinded him, but had travelled further through his body and he was unable to move out of the house. Finally, he was driven to his bed. He was only fifty-six years of age. What a tragedy! Yet I don't remember him complaining, although he suffered terrible agony.

My father and I became great pals. We exchanged many confidences. He listened to my boyish plans about the future with patience, and I to his many adventures in the army and out of it. He was extraordinarily broad-minded. He provided the money for the books I read to him and insisted that they be my own choice. Occasionally, he would try me out on Shakespeare or Dickens. When I looked like being bored he would send me off to purchase a penny dreadful or *Buffalo Bill*. He never tired of Mayne Reid, Marryat or Henty.

Then he died and he carried with him to the grave my childhood. I knew that none could take his place. I don't believe I was anxious that anyone should. Although nigh forty-four years separated my father and I, he had easily travelled backwards so that we two might understand each other. His blind eyes had always followed me as I moved about his room with that curious unseeing understanding and affection which I had come to feel and will treasure till the end of my days. He was a great fellow.

I wasn't more than a week home from Dublin when my brother managed to procure me a start with the printing firm which employed him. I was put to an embossing machine. I was shifted from that after I had missed jamming the printer's hand by a hair's breadth. Then I tackled the bronzing, one of the most sickening jobs I ever worked at. The wages were three shillings a week. About fifty years ago a labouring man working in Belfast was lucky to carry home sixteen shillings as a week's wages. But tobacco was only threepence an ounce then, a pint of porter twopence, and a bakery bap, which would have given a navvy a square meal, a penny.

Factory life didn't suit me. The glamour of Phoenix Park isn't easily extinguished. The gloomy, dust-laden rooms of the printing house created an atmosphere of misery to my youthful mind. The yellow lime-washed walls gave the place a cell-like appearance. I had a feeling of being smothered every time I entered the building, and felt like screaming and dashing outside into the street.

It wasn't that I was workshy. All youngsters are over-eager to earn a wage. It makes them feel as if they've grown into manhood. I heard there was a message boy wanted in a butcher's shop on the Ormeau Road, so I took a day off and applied for the job. The owner was a quiet-looking individual with a religious background—Methodist, I believe.

"What Sunday school do you attend?" he questioned.

I lied without any qualms. He seemed to be satisfied. I still retained a distinctive southern accent which for many years held me under suspicion of being a Catholic. I soon learned, when applying for a job in certain quarters, to state my denomination without being asked. It cleared the air somewhat. I don't believe for a moment it got you the job, for I have yet to meet the employer who chooses a man to work for him merely because that man may have a conscience.

I collared the job in any case, with an addition of sixpence to my former wage. The sixpence was recompense for a further six hours added to my working week. The one part of my new job I disliked most was having to carry on until eleven o'clock on a Saturday night. After the first week I realised that sixpence was a poor enough bribe for the sacrifice.

One afternoon, I had no messages to do, so the boss thought he would give me some useful work in the meantime. I was put to the sausage machine. It was sticky, clammy, loathsome work for a youngster. The sausages had a deplorable habit of exploding in one's face without warning. I took an intense dislike to that machine and considered it my duty to terminate its usefulness. I placed a hambone inside along with the sausage meat. The machine gave a couple of grunts before it exploded. When the boss came on the scene, he too exploded and I was fired.

I was staying with one of my sisters since my father's death. She was some six years my senior, and together we rented a small room in the Ormeau Road area. I realised she needed my wages to keep things going, so there was nothing for it but to get another job, and to get it quick.

I heard there was a chance in a heddle and reed factory, beside the Great Northern Railway Station, and applied immediately. When I found the wages had increased another sixpence to four shillings, I was feeling at the top of the world. I might have held on to the job long enough but for an incident which happened when I was there about three months.

Spinsters, especially if they were getting on in years, had to remain at work until they actually fell off their feet with exhaustion, or age made it impossible to carry on. And fifty was old age in those days. One morning, an aged woman employee slid to the floor of the factory and died quietly. She was carried into the storeroom on a wooden frame and laid there until the ambulance should arrive. I was detailed to keep the rats away from the body. It was a horrible job for a youngster. I was scared stiff myself—and it wasn't through fear of rats.

There was a vacancy for a youth in a yarn store in the neighbourhood of Bedford Street, which was the centre of the linen trade. The following morning, I put in an appearance at the store. After the usual inquiry regarding references and an unbelieving smile when I stated my religion, I got the job. I received something like a shock when the boss informed me my wages would be six shillings a week, but it was nothing compared to the shock I had coming to me when I discovered how the six shillings was to be earned.

At the time I write about, the entire commercial method of transport was by horse and van. This seemed to be rather expensive to the linen merchants, so they instituted a cheaper, though much slower method. Boys, aged between fourteen and sixteen, were employed as 'porters'. Their job was to wheel a strongly-built handcart, packed with anything up to thirty hundred-weight of flax or linen, from one warehouse to another.

It was impossible to drag this along with the hands alone, so a rope was slung round the shoulders and attached to the cart. It was murder, but I needed the six shillings.

II

I hauled the handcart about for three solid months before the seeds of discontent which had been growing on me took shape and I determined to make a change no matter what it cost. The change came about this way.

The office hands loaded the cart to its limit with orders that the load was to be delivered to a mill on the Falls Road, at the top end of Albert Street. It was uphill pulling. I wasn't more than fifteen at the time and what little strength I possessed was expended half way up the hill. The rope was actually cutting into my flesh with the strain and my arms had almost ceased to function before I collapsed and lay across the shafts of the handcart. The cart itself was hauling me back down the hill when a couple of men came to my assistance.

"God," one of them exclaimed, "that's no load for a child to haul about!"

"If he was my youngster," the other fellow added, "I'd have the bloody man's life that would send him on a job like that!"

I had changed my whole outlook on life inside an hour. A child in mind and spirit had dragged that handcart up the hill. Returning with the empty cart, I was cursing the boss for using me as he would a beast of burden; I was cursing the system which allowed a boss the use of a human being for the purpose. It was more dignifying to be flogged for breaking the law. I could almost visualise the boss arranging another journey by telephone: "I'll have the boy take it round in the handcart."

I said to myself, "Hell! He won't!"

And he didn't. I lifted my wages that evening, and without informing any of my brothers or sisters, went off that night to Glasgow. The fare to Glasgow cost four shillings, which left me with two shillings to squander as I wished. How I intended to live when I got to Glasgow never worried me. I would get work and all would be well.

Aboard the boat, I met another lad travelling with a similar purpose—to get a job. He was a big, husky country lad of seventeen and he offered to mate up with me. I was willing. We had twelve shillings between us. He paid for two mugs of tea and I supplied a couple of soda farls I had brought with me.

Landing in Glasgow, we immediately set out on our search. We made application at half a dozen factories before we hunted up an eating house. We paid fourpence each for a coarse but hefty dinner. When evening came, we were still searching for a job. Then we inquired about somewhere to lodge for the night. We were directed to a model lodging house down by the docks. The bed cost me another fourpence. We managed a light meal at a cost of twopence.

In the main room, we foregathered with the other boarders. They were dull company. There was a docker who seemed to have brought the docks with him; he was continuously munching corn picked up along the wharf side. Beside him sat a navvy who looked like a pensioned grave-digger.

Nat, which was my chum's name, wasn't conspicuously gentle in elbowing seats for the two of us in the wide semi-circle of rags and dirt huddled around the stove. Conversation was as ragged as the company. Now and then, a member of the circle would make a chance remark to his neighbour. The stony look he would receive in reply froze him into silence.

To move in one's seat was to lose a cubic inch of space, and as one's allotment wasn't measured in proportion, you remained perfectly steady.

Later, in the dormitory, Nat and I enjoyed ourselves. Two rows of single beds ran up the centre of the room; behind these, taking up wall and window space, were small cubicles. The cubicles cost twopence more than the centre beds. A couple of gas jets blinked a blue flame at either end of the room. The place stank. So did some of the occupants. Round about midnight, the first drunk arrived. He wanted to sing. In fact, he did sing.

His rendering of 'Bonny Mary of Argyle' brought a chorus of foul oaths down on his head, but we might as well have tried to drown a duck in water. Another drunk, who had fallen asleep, woke up with a grunt, lay over the side of his bed to clear his throat—and stomach, spat out, and joined in with the 'Sailor's Farewell'. I was too young to comprehend the gist of the ballad, but it was pretty hot. It was bordering on three in the morning before any of us got a wink of sleep.

The next morning we were out again, scouring the city for work. I was fast losing enthusiasm. Back in Belfast, I had it drilled into me that Glasgow was an open market—work for the mere picking up. There wasn't the butt end of a Woodbine to be picked up, let alone work. Nat and I went into an eating house, towards dinner time, and I spent my last fourpence on a meal. Coming out of the place, I walked a few paces up the street and waited on Nat. The footpath was crowded with people, whom it was quite interesting to watch passing.

I walked back to the eating house to pick up Nat, but I saw no sign of him. The waitress informed me he had followed me out. I rushed outside and raced up and down the street in a panic. He had disappeared. I hadn't a penny left to my name. I was depending on Nat paying my bed that night.

I don't believe he meant to walk out on me. He had probably missed me in the crowded thoroughfare and moved off in a different direction to where I was waiting. I hung about the door of the lodging house that night as a forlorn hope. At the finish, I was forced to sleep in a shed beside the docks.

The next day, I had nothing to eat and at night returned to the shed. The following day was a repetition. I was really starving in the second greatest city of the United Kingdom. On the third day, a docker sensed something wrong and slipped a couple of coppers into my hand. I bought two immense buns and a bottle of lemonade. Inside ten minutes, I thought I was going to die. I was doubled up with pain. But I came round all right.

I stood by the Belfast boat that night praying someone would recognise me and pay my passage. A man, some acquaintance of one of my sisters, halted half way up the gangway, then turned and spoke to me.

"What are ye doing here, Carnduff?" he inquired.

I hadn't the faintest idea who the man was, but I gave him the whole tale. He was a decent chap. After paying my passage back, he supplied me with a good meal aboard, and made me promise to let my people know all about it when we arrived in Belfast.

I haven't visited Glasgow since.

Chapter Two

'The Pass Clan'

Police baton charges were quite a common occurrence in the early 1900s. The police themselves were never popular with either Protestant or Catholic crowds and, often enough, they had to face either ways when a riot was proceeding. In those days, the old RIC only carried firearms on ceremonial parades. Today, the Royal Ulster Constabulary are armed to the teeth: rifle and bayonet, revolver and baton, and tommy gun when needed. My first collision with the police happened on the relief of Ladysmith celebrations.

When the news of the relief of Ladysmith was received in Belfast, the entire population downed tools and crowded the main thoroughfares to demonstrate. There was a continuous procession of cheering crowds along the principal streets. This continued hour after hour without cessation.

As the evening wore on, the procession was augmented with dozens of brass and fife-and-drum bands. I was following a brass band in the procession along Royal Avenue when a shower of stones dropped amongst the crowd, thrown from the direction of Kent Street. Kent Street, being a Catholic quarter, was naturally pro-Boer.

There was an immediate rush by the crowd in this direction, but the police were waiting for this eventuality. They knew the likely hot spots when Protestant crowds decided to demonstrate. So I record my first baton charge. There was a panic when the police charged and I came out of the scrimmage minus one canvas shoe and my cap. Still, I enjoyed the excitement and went over my adventure with great gusto when I finally arrived home, somewhere about two in the morning.

I have often been asked by Englishmen why Belfast people are so quarrelsome amongst themselves. Normally, they are no more quarrelsome than similar communities. Politics alone would have a poor chance of creating civil strife in Belfast without a background of religious animosity to keep it alive. There wasn't a solitary head broken during the 1902 by-election in South Belfast because the two opposing parties were Protestant. In the West Division, where a Catholic usually faced a Protestant opponent, the place was in turmoil for weeks, during and after the election. There is very little changed, even to the present day.

The same vicious system which separates the children into religious groups to create suspicion and misunderstanding, splits the adult population into similar communities. There is always the inevitable demarcation line between a Catholic and Protestant quarter of the city. When trouble starts, it is there the police concentrate. In the suburbs, where the population is somewhat mixed, there is generally peace and orderliness. That is, if the people are left to themselves.

Life, for young working-class people in 1900, was somewhat empty of entertainment. There were no cinemas, few organised playing fields and, with the exception of religious societies, no attempt to induce the youth of the city to fit themselves into healthy and useful citizens. So we grouped ourselves into 'clans'.

In my youth, the 'clan' system in Belfast grew out of a code built up on mutual protection. It was dangerous for a youth between the ages of twelve and eighteen to wander out of his own district alone. He would be set upon and beaten up by young boys of his own age. To be quite fair, these youths were by no means of the criminal type; but, oh gosh, were they tough!

These 'clans' had their own particular hunting ground, and had a rendezvous in some back street in their own district, which made it difficult for the police to locate them.

My brother, Wilfred, had some connection with a clan from York Street, 'The Forty Thieves'. These 'Forty Thieves' would invade the centre thoroughfares of the city on Saturday night, and every clan within sight would disappear until the 'all clear' was sounded.

The 'Cronji Clan' were recognisable by their black-and-white check caps, and foregathered somewhere in the neighbourhood of the Falls Road. The 'Cronji Clan' and 'Forty Thieves' were bitter enemies and their battle cries were often the signal for some of the fiercest sectarian riots in the city.

The 'Bushrangers' held sway in what was once the red lamp district of the city, behind the present St. Anne's Cathedral. How they came by the name I don't remember. I only know that we smaller fry kept a weather eye open for their appearance in the streets.

Another crowd of hooligans of local repute went by the title of 'The Bogey Clan'. There was a row on the Crumlin Road, one evening, when knives were used. A youth died from his injuries. The police swooped down on the Bogey Clan, a few days later, and a number of them were placed behind iron bars for the good of their souls and the peace of the city.

About this time, I was developing into a pretty wild sample of budding manhood myself. The fault was all my own. There were nine of us grouped together who made up 'The Pass Clan'. I joined the clan as much for protection as devilment. We were as tough a crowd of young bucks as could be found in the city. Our particular aversion was 'Catholics'. We ambushed them, jibed them, slaughtered them when opportunity came our way. Yet many of these 'corner boys' became useful citizens in after years.

My own chum, who was as ignorant of education as any illiterate, is now a full-blown Presbyterian minister in western Canada. Another set up business, a few years ago, on a leading thoroughfare of the city and, by all accounts, he is building up a promising concern. Two others, who were the mischief for getting us all into trouble, are foremen in their respective trades, while yet another occupies a position as Timekeeper in the shipyards. During the first Great War, five of the 'clan' joined the services, two reaching the rank of sergeant.

This picture of Belfast in the early 1900s may be lapped up by some of my readers who have no great love for the city's history or reputation. Yet Belfast in those days was no better or worse than any other seaport in the British Isles. In fact, what I saw of Glasgow, Liverpool, Cardiff, Sunderland, fails to cause me any grief in regard to the social life of my own city in the early days of this century. Even Dublin had little to be proud of when I knew it best. It's just that I was born and brought up here and poked my nose into places I had been taught to side step, but didn't.

Chapter Three

'Sweating and half-timers'

I

King Edward VII paid a visit to the city about this time. His Majesty was to open the new City Hall and unveil a statue to his mother, Queen Victoria. It was the first visit of a reigning sovereign to Belfast for many years and the population went crazy. It is my earliest recollection of Belfast pageantry on a large scale and, to me, that particular occasion has yet to be beaten. The citizens went carnival mad, for I distinctly remember a large crowd gathering at Castle Junction, towards 4 am on the morning of the visit, to sing the National Anthem.

It often puzzles me why Ulstermen adopt such patriotic zeal on occasions like this. I have witnessed three Royal visits to the city and, on each occasion, the population went wild in their eagerness to demonstrate their loyalty.

The Belfastman, individually, is not demonstrative. He is rather the reverse. You've got to work him up to it, and it's hard work at that. I think it's the antagonism of the Belfast Catholic to anything English which rouses the Protestant population to excessive patriotism, rather than admiration for Englishmen themselves.

In the early 1900s, Belfast was rapidly rising into prominence as a great seaport town. It was growing in industrial importance but was still a backward city in regard to civic reforms. The streets were ugly and slums too numerous. The main highways were paved with square sets, and working-class streets retained their cobbled sidewalks. Carts rumbled over the paving stones and horse-drawn trams thundered along the main thoroughfares with deafening detonations. To journey from one part of the city to another was an ordeal—it took time and patience.

The Queen's Island shipbuilding yard had produced the largest tonnage of new shipping in one single year. Workman & Clark's shipyard equalled the record a few years later. Linen manufacture was at its peak. Gallagher's tobacco factory was easily the largest of its kind in the world, as was York Street Flax Spinning Mill. The Belfast Ropework Co had little competition.

Yet the Belfast worker received the lowest standard rate of wages in the

United Kingdom. The labouring class was bordering on starvation. I know, because I was one myself. Charitable institutions simply basked in the sunshine of their own importance. Old and infirm men and women, unable to work longer, trudged wearily up to the gates of the workhouse. There was no alternative.

Much as their grown-up children were anxious to support them, they themselves were barely able to provide for their own families. Wives as well as husbands were compelled to work out if they wished to live in any sort of comfort. This is a sad and sordid picture. Nevertheless, it is a true one.

Those were the days of 'sweating' and 'half-timers'. A child of twelve years was allowed to work three days in a mill and spend the other two at school. A boy's wages for the three days was two shillings, and a penny as an inducement to become a useful worker. He commenced work at 6 am and finished at 6 pm. If he missed a day at work, he was compelled to attend school two days as punishment.

Of the 65,000 persons employed in the mills in 1904 more than six per cent were children under the age of thirteen. In 1833 a factory act was passed allowing children between the ages of nine and thirteen to labour no more than nine hours a day. As late as 1906, they were still allowed to employ children between the ages of twelve and fourteen to work nine hours a day. They were checking in a 6.30 am and finished their day's work at 6 pm in the evening, with three quarter of an hour's break for breakfast and dinner. Saturday was a half day.

During that particular period the wages of adult workers over eighteen were paid the lowest rates in the kingdom. Spinners earned ten shillings and sixpence, reelers eleven and threepence, and weavers eleven and sixpence weekly. Shawls were the only outside covering, coats and hats were unknown, except for the weavers, who were considered above the ordinary millworker.

Clubs were formed in the mills to give the youngsters an opportunity to supply themselves with boots. Instalments were collected at the rate of threepence a week. Mill girls were known by the name of 'shawlies'. Few of them could afford to wear any other covering garment. Linen was doled out for stitching by warerooms to married women in their own homes. The remuneration was shocking. A sister-in-law of my own worked until 2 am in the morning to earn sixpence. She had a baby and two older children to look after at the same time.

It was in this putrid prosperity that, as a boy, I began to write doggerel, which afterwards, long afterwards, developed into minor poetry.

II

On my return from the Glasgow fiasco, I managed to get reinstated in my former job as light porter with the linen merchant but I was still restless and, on a certain Saturday, some months later, with my week's wages in my pocket, I sailed for Liverpool. I had the devil's own luck on these excursions in search for work. After a fortnight boiling billy cans for navvies and doing odd messages, I saved enough to get me back home, disillusioned and completely fed up with life.

I hated to sponge on my relatives but there wasn't any other way out. Gosh, but I did feel my position keenly! It was an awful predicament for a young fellow of sixteen to be in, depending on what he could cadge to keep life warm in him.

I commenced to frequent the Public Libraries, reading every English poet and essayist I could lay hands on. Shelley, Keats, Crabbe, Byron and Moore were followed by a host of modern poets. I was soon suffering from poetic hysteria. I grew into a surly, muttering, mentally-deranged idiot during the day and a storehouse of nightmares at night.

I waded through Dante's 'Inferno' and came out of it more dead than alive. When I had finished Milton's 'Paradise Lost and Regained', it took me another week to regain my reason. When I had completed Shakespeare, I was well on my way to the asylum. I began taking long walks into the country, not in search of beauty, but to talk myself into a state of mental collapse. And I nearly succeeded.

A neighbour of my sister's, who was foreman in the stereo room of the now defunct *Ulster Echo*, a Belfast evening paper, offered me a job as assistant under him. That kindly gesture from a perfect stranger practically saved my life. I started the following morning. My wages were seventeen shillings a week. A big increase on my former remuneration. The work was pretty strenuous and difficult to follow, but I was young and intelligent and, in a few weeks, I had become useful enough to be worth my wage.

I have always found printers and joiners rather above the average in general intelligence amongst workers. I don't mean they are more efficient as tradesmen, but in their general knowledge, outside their ordinary vocations. My new work was interesting and instructive.

I had opportunities to study most London newspapers and magazines without the usual expense attached to this recreation and my fellow-workers were the most argumentative set of men I have ever worked with.

We had periodic spells in between the editions which were spent gambling, in one form or another. They were a great bunch of cardsharpers and would stake the very shirt off their back in any sort of gamble. Week after week, I lost everything but my overalls, but I learned a lot and it was great fun—to the winner.

The *Ulster Echo*, which was founded in 1874 as an evening newspaper, was sponsored by the Ulster Presbyterian community, and had been Liberal in politics prior to the Home Rule split. When I joined the staff, in 1906, it was Tory to its backbone. That is probably the reason why its circulation never rose beyond a few thousand. There were three other Tory papers in competition in the city. During the First World War, it struggled for existence, but finally gave up the ghost in 1916.

Chapter Four

'A Protestant of good standing'

I

Outside Ireland, Orangeism is badly misrepresented. The Catholic press in Ireland is rather biased in its reports when civil commotions give it an opportunity to lay the blame for all the political and religious upheavals in Ireland at the door of the Orange Society.

Granted that it doesn't take a great deal of abuse to rouse Orangemen to prepare for action, it must be recognised that a minority, in any country, have for ever to be on guard. And where Irishmen are concerned, it is little odds what colours they fly; one phrase spoken in contempt can begin a row which might finally be quelled after a new cemetery has been opened to satisfy their honour and glory.

Still, having been a member of the order for many years myself, I am afraid the reader will have to accept my opinions regarding Orangeism as being sympathetic to their ideals. My family have been connected with the Orange Institution since its inception, one hundred and fifty-seven years ago.

I admit that secret societies, especially when those societies are actuated in their activities because of religion, are a danger rather than an asset to any country. There are circles in the Orange Order which are secret in their deliberations; that is, where no minutes are recorded of the meetings.

In every Orange lodge, from the opening to the closing ceremony, there is not an item of business which is not recorded in the written minutes of the lodge book. There is absolutely nothing secret in lodge reports that any member could be called into account for, except, of course, conduct within the lodge itself.

Catholics in Ireland have their own societies, secret and otherwise, which they have a perfect right to join. I know nothing of these societies so have no opinion to offer in regard to their activities. It may be there are too many semi-religious organisations interfering in Irish politics. Party politics are troublesome enough in any community, but when religious prejudices enter into the game, sane and reasonable argument is at a disadvantage.

Discipline in Orange lodges is almost dictatorial. The Worshipful Master of the lodge is not alone the power behind the throne, he is the throne. His permission has to be sought to enter the lodge room, to speak in the various discussions, even to leave the room. That is why Orangemen make the best and most orderly trade unionists. No matter how they may dislike the Worshipful Master's ruling, they obey it.

The first Book of Rules printed for the guidance of Orange lodges contained these principles:

"... to aid and assist all loyal subjects of every religious persuasion by protecting them from violence and oppression.

"... his disposition should be humane and compassionate, his behaviour kind and courteous. He should love rational and improving society."

There is no attempt in these early rules and ordinances to direct the Orangeman's mind into particular party political groups. It merely insists that he be a Protestant of good standing. To my knowledge, these rules are still the fundamentals of the Orange Society. These rules may have been broken on many occasions, but that does not alter the principles of the body.

I have no wish to write a treatise in defence of Orangeism. I may be somewhat biased towards the order because of my upbringing and family connections. Still, one may live in an atmosphere of religion and not be religious. I have known publicans to serve beer and spirits practically all their life and yet remain teetotallers.

In 1900, when I had finished my education in the Hibernian school and returned home to Belfast to live with my father, my knowledge of Orangeism could have been improved upon. I was soon instructed in regard to my ignorance by my brothers. Protestantism and the Orange Society meant more to them than their daily bread and butter. In fact, it was their bread and butter.

Conscience, mode of life, their opinions on public affairs, even their family life was mixed up with the importance of keeping Popery at a comfortable distance. I stumbled about in this bigoted atmosphere wondering what the whole thing was about.

My father, who possessed a fairly good education for his times, was broad-minded in nearly everything but politics. He was an out-and-out Tory, blind to even the merest notion of reforms in ways of life or conditions, in case there might be a hint of Liberalism in any changes. How I managed to develop an attitude of independence and an opinion of my own is a mystery to me.

The Orange Society was founded away back in 1795. It began with the people. There can be no question regarding this fact. Agricultural workers and linen weavers made up its first membership. Very soon, the gentry and landowning class realised the possibilities of using the organisation as a first line of defence for their own particular interests.

Once the order had grown in numbers and was strong enough to be counted a political force in the country, peers and gentry, who, hitherto, had looked with suspicion on the proletariat background of the movement, now came forward and soon occupied the dominating positions.

During the month of September, 1795, religious animosity had increased to a ferocity unequalled in Irish history. Outrage and murder were common to all parts. In Ulster, this culminated in a pitched battle between the Protestant and Catholic peasantry in County Armagh. A three-day conflict took place at Loughgall, a small townland some miles distant from Portadown, both parties being armed to the teeth with shotguns and pikes. After seventy or eighty men had been killed and hundreds wounded, the Catholic party were driven off.

After the battle, a number of Protestants gathered at the home of one of their number and a warrant was signed creating the first Orange lodge. At first, the lodges consisted of members of the established church alone, the Presbyterians holding aloof. During the 1798 rebellion, the Orangemen were formed into corps of yeomen and the cleavance between them and the Presbyterian rebels became still wider.

In 1800, after the Act of Union, the Presbyterians weakened in their opposition to the Orange Society and by the time Dan O'Connell had become leader of the Catholic party, they had joined forces with their fellow Protestants to make the order a powerful force in the country.

There is much more to it than I have explained but this brief outline will give the reader a fair idea of the origin and rise of the society in Ulster. Many generations of my own family—five, at least—have been connected with the Orange Order. One of our family treasures, in my possession, is the Orange sash worn by my grandfather over a century ago.

In 1900, practically every male belonging to the Protestant industrial classes was a member of the society. Both my brothers, Arthur and Wilfred, had joined the brotherhood. I knew it would only be a matter of time before I too would be initiated. The blessed thing was in my blood long before I was the age for joining.

Whilst I was in school in Dublin, an Orangeman, Arthur Trew, who had spent the early part of his life in New York, had organised a militant Protestant organisation in Belfast. He was a little man with a limp, and a squeaky voice that carried yards beyond his platform. If ever there was a born agitator, that man was Trew.

The Grand Orange Lodge looked upon Trew with suspicion, but the rank and file of the order backed him to a man. Still, the majority of the Grand Lodge were well-to-do merchants, Justices of the Peace and clergymen, having little in common with Trew or his supporters.

The South African war was still in the news when the Belfast Catholics organised a Corpus Christi celebration, the proposed procession to pass through the Falls Road district. Arthur Trew and his Belfast Protestant Association declared they would hold a counter-demonstration. The authorities banned the proposed counter-demonstration. Trew refused to accept the authority's ruling and a pleasant little row developed, many persons being injured, police as well as civilians. On this occasion, the Shankill Road was the scene of hostilities.

Trew was arrested and, after a trial, sent to prison for twelve months. The Protestant Association increased its membership by thousands. My chum, Jimmie Parker, and I joined the Sandy Row branch. It was usual for the association to hold mass meetings every Sunday afternoon at the Custom House steps, facing the dockside.

After Arthur Trew's arrest, the Sunday meetings increased to vast proportions. Tom Sloan, a shipyard cement worker, donned the mantle of Arthur and trouble piled up for the Tory leaders. Up till this time, the Tory Party in Belfast was easily cock of the walk. The Liberal Party was of little account, except in some country districts, and the Socialist movement was in its infancy.

William Johnson, the member for South Belfast, died, causing a parliamentary vacancy. Sandy Row was part of the constituency and the Orangemen were in revolt. Johnson had fought the Tories in his early days as an independent conservative and given them some severe defeats. Later, he had slackened in his opposition. But the Orangemen, who had revolted on his behalf thirty years previously, remembered the battles and were prepared to fight again.

The Tories put up a County Down landowner as their candidate. The Protestant Association collected subscriptions to fight the election and backed Tom Sloan as their champion. Members of parliament were not with the Independents. It so happened that one of my cousins was Worshipful Master of an independent lodge, so, with his backing, I was initiated into Sandy Row True Blues, Independent Loyal Orange Lodge No. 5. There was a bit of a family row and little brother love between us for some months.

I became an enthusiastic member of the lodge and found my fellow lodgemen a likable lot, friendly and sincere in their belief. Most of the members were artisans of one trade or another, intelligent and reasonable in discussion but fiercely partisan in the Protestant cause.

A national spirit was creeping into Ulster politics at this time and I discovered many of these Orangemen intensely Irish in their outlook. So much so that, about 1905, during a demonstration at Magheramourne, a small village above Larne, they issued a manifesto pledging their support to any movement which would improve the well-being of their native land.

The manifesto was signed by the Grand Master, R. Lindsay Crawford; the Rev. D.D. Boyle, a Ballymoney Presbyterian clergyman; Tom Sloan MP and the Grand Secretary, Richard Braithwaite. It was issued at Magheramourne on the 13th of July, 1905.

The manifesto was dedicated in bold print:

"... TO ALL IRISHMEN WHOSE COUNTRY STANDS FIRST IN THEIR AFFECTIONS. FROM THE INDEPENDENT ORANGEMEN OF IRELAND.

"... Castle government stands self-condemned. All parties are agreed as to the necessity of sweeping reforms in the government and administration of Ireland. It only remains to be determined on what lines reform is to proceed and what part Irishmen are to play in bringing it about. On the willingness and ability of Irishmen to co-operate in carrying out reasonable reforms, their own country will rest their claim to a more extended form of self-government.

"... Government by the people for the people is a democratic principle, limited only in its application by the ability of the people to govern.

"... Unionism is likewise a discredited creed. National ideas were once more to be sacrificed on the altar of sectarianism and Home Ruler and Unionist alike duped by their leaders.

"... We do not trust either of the English parties on any of the questions that divide Ireland, and we are satisfied that both Liberals and Tories will continue in the future, as they have done in the past, to play off Irish Protestants and Nationalists against each other, to the prejudice of their country.

"... In an Ireland in which Protestant and Roman Catholic stand sullen and discontented, it is not too much to hope that they will reconsider their position, and, in their common trials, unite on a true basis of Nationality.

"... The higher claims of our distracted country have been too long neglected in the strife of party and of greed. The man who cannot rise above the trammels of party and of sect on a national issue is a foe to Nationality and human freedom."

The final statement in the manifesto takes the form of a prophecy rather than that of an opinion. "... We foresee a time in Irish history when thoughtful men on both sides will come to realise that the Irish question is not made up of Union or Repeal; that not in acts of parliament nor in their repeal lies the hope and salvation of our country, so much as in the mutual inclination of Irish hearts and minds along the common plane of Nationality—a Nationality that binds the people together in the school, in the workshop, and in the Senate in the promotion of what has long been neglected, the material interests of our native land, and the increased wealth and happiness of her people."

Before I leave the manifesto, I think it would be a mistake if I were to omit one particular paragraph which dealt with the past rather than the present or future, and which certainly laid the blame of Ireland's political blunders upon Irishmen themselves:

"... Looking across the vista of years since the passing of the Act of Union, we are forced to the conclusion that the lamentable condition of Ireland is mainly attributable to the false conception of nationality that prevails amongst rulers and people ... that Irishmen have never learned to think nationally, but have invoked, with disastrous results, the intervention of external influences, instead of appealing to the latent spirit of Irish patriotism and citizenship."

The manifesto caused an upheaval in Irish politics, and even in the ranks of the Independents there was some opposition. A meeting was held in the Exhibition Hall to ratify the manifesto. Only Orangemen were allowed admittance. At times, the meeting grew a bit stormy. On a final vote, there were few dissentients. Most of us came out of the meeting determined to put the words of the manifesto into effect through political channels.

It was believed, and I think rightly so, that Lindsay Crawford was the real spirit behind the manifesto, and that Tom Sloan MP, was rather lukewarm in his support. The following year, during the 1906 General Election, Sloan did repudiate much of his earlier support.

In any case, Lindsay Crawford was eventually elected Imperial Grand Master of the order, much to the discomfort of Tom Sloan and his admirers in the new order.

II

Bickerings amongst the members in regard to manifesto brought the progress of the movement to a standstill, whilst the fierce opposition of the parent order was beginning to wean the weaker individual members from its ranks. The official press, too, added their weight to the abuse and victimisation which was now applied to the rank and file of the Independents.

There was something like thirty-five Independent lodges in Belfast district during the 12th of July demonstration in 1907, and probably double that number in north Antrim. In the outlying districts of Armagh and Down and Derry, there may have been thirty more lodges.

During the 1906 General Election, the Independents showed their teeth in north Antrim and South Belfast by supporting two independent candidates, both of whom defeated the local Tory nominee. Tom Sloan was returned for South Belfast by 816 votes and R.G. Glendinning with a majority of 788.

Most Catholics look upon the Orange Order as a bulwark of landlordism and the Tory Party. This is all wrong. Time after time, during the history of the Order, the rank and file have rebelled against their leaders. At the Act of Union, Orangemen in the main held aloof from interfering with the movement. There were as many for as against. The Grand Lodge tried to sway the order towards accepting the Act in its entirety, yet no less than thirty-six lodges assembled at Armagh and declared themselves against the Union and a further thirteen lodges in County Fermanagh echoed their sentiments.

In 1907, during the Belfast dockers strike, Lindsay Crawford presided over a meeting of the strikers on the Falls Road, when Jim Larkin was present. The Tory press thundered out a protest at an Orangeman occupying a platform in the heart of a Catholic district. The Independent Orangemen not alone supported their Grand Master, but they passed a resolution at their 12th of July demonstration at Shaw's Bridge, in support of the strikers. This was the wording of the resolution: "That this mass meeting of the citizens of Belfast condemns the action of those who refuse to recognise the principles of Trade Unionism, and to which is due the deplorable strike that at present paralyses trade and inflicts much suffering upon the workers of Belfast."

To be more practical, they raised a collection round their members and supporters at the Field itself.

The Grand Lodge of the Independents, encouraged by Tom Sloan MP, who by this time had become jealous of Crawford's popularity, expelled the Grand Master from the Order. With many other labour sympathisers, I resigned as a protest, rejoining the order some years later. Sloan was eventually defeated in the General Election of 1910 and the Independents gradually disappeared as a political force in Ulster.

Looking back now, I believe the decline of the Independents was a tragedy to our country. The movement was not unsimilar to that of the Irish Volunteer period of 1782. The Independent Order was, like its predecessor of 1782, a product of Protestant Belfast. Its reign lasted for a like period. There were possibilities in the broad outlook of its members upon the national and religious conscience of Ireland.

The movement failed because the cultural classes were subservient to the political caucus who ruled in Ulster. They are, and will remain so until a new generation will arise to face the realities of public life and social morals. In the north, it is power politics that rule the conscience of the people. In the south, it is the church that guides the public conscience.

My opinion may count for little when weighed against that of credited students of religious and political science. Yet if we ordinary citizens of a carved-up nation do not express an intelligent interest in our country, what future is left for a peaceful and united Ireland?

Chapter Five

'These Sons of Ulster marching'

I drifted away from politics and became interested in other matters. The fact suddenly dawned upon me that half of this talk of democratic idealism was mere piffle to win popular support for one party or the other. For fully seven years, I had used up my spare hours and nearly ruined a strong pair of youthful lungs to further a cause which was now shattered because a few men at the head of affairs squabbled for leadership.

I had subscribed liberally to the funds out of my small earnings and worked laboriously without any hope of recompense. I had come to realise that if the world was to be made a cleaner and happier place for humanity, political idealism was less than a forlorn hope.

The Orange lodge is part of an Ulsterman's life. He grows up with it. He may have liberal or labour tendencies which clash with the Tory background of Orangeism and, within the political life of Ulster itself, may oppose those who use it as a bannister to political power.

But let any outsider criticise or abuse Orangeism because it is an Ulster product and he immediately becomes a defender of all it stands for, despite the fact that he himself has little use for it as a political weapon.

The Boyne anniversary, held annually on the 12th of July, is a celebration few Ulster Protestants would care to see banned, no matter what their political outlook may be. The hundreds of bands and five miles long procession of marching Orangemen with flaunting banners and varied coloured sashes, seems far removed from any semblance of political or religious rancour.

Watching these sons of Ulster marching in military formation, sturdy and strong in their belief that they alone are the rightful champions of civil and religious liberty in their native land, one cannot but admire and respect their dignity and orderliness, irrespective whether their cause be just or unjust. Even if ritual and ceremony is exploited to an extreme degree by Orangemen, they are no worse defaulters from realism or sane argument than most orthodox Christian churches.

Time and again have Belfast Orangemen kicked the traces when politicians have thought to deviate them, with impunity, from their old-time independence of party politics. Today, the most popular Orange districts in Belfast, the Shankill and Woodvale Roads, are represented in the northern parliament by two Orange members who are the bitterest opponents of the Tory Party in Ulster and, in every election, have fought them to a standstill. In fact, during the 1949 General Election in the north, the official party thought it convenient to allow both an unopposed return.

The constitution of the Orange Society is supremely democratic. The private lodges elect representatives to the district lodge, who in turn elect the county lodge. The Imperial Grand Lodge is formed out of representatives elected from the several counties. Any private member who has passed through the degrees can travel up to the highest lodge. Few of the ordinary members ever reach that exalted position but there is nothing in the rules or obligations to deter them.

True, during the latter end of the last century, peers, generals and dignitaries of the church made common cause with the brethren in their opposition to the Catholic Church. The landowning class needed such stalwarts in those days to counteract the influence of the Land League and reform movements in Ireland. What would Captain Boycott and his type have done without their moral support?

Once the ownership of the land had passed out of their hands, peers and landlords had no further use for the lodges and, today, they are an unknown quantity in the ranks of the Orange Society. The high officials of the order, at the present time, are merchants and small traders, who in the old days were small fry compared to My Lord and his doughty squires.

Many of the Orange lodges in Belfast use their occupations and trades in the various titles of the lodges. Take these lodge titles as an example: Bakers LOL, Paviors LOL, Mechanics LOL, Shipwrights LOL, Great Northern LOL—which is composed of employees of the Great Northern Railway. There is another lodge, recently founded, Press LOL, composed entirely of printers. Other lodges carry the title on their banners of the various churches where the lodge originated.

The Catholic press in Éire, as well as in Northern Ireland, is too fond of applying the adjective 'Orange' to every type of mob violence or political commotion which may crop up in any neighbourhood where Ulster Protestants predominate. There may be odd Orangemen mixed up in the row, or their may not, it matters little to the militant Catholic journalist so that he may procure copy stigmatising Orangeism as a danger to the community.

Probably, this opinion of mine will cause some readers to throw this book down and cry: "Bigotry! The man's a propagandist for the Orange Society!"

Well, go ahead. I can't compel you to read, but I can challenge you to give the work an even break before you condemn it as a piece of Orange propaganda.

Chapter Six

'A rumpus down at the docks'

It was in the year 1906 I began work in the stereo department of the now defunct *Ulster Echo*. The stereo plant and printing machine was of the old Victory type—ancient and cumbersome. Three or four thousand copies of a four-page paper an hour would be a record—if the machine held out. Occasionally, it had a habit of trying to hamstring me with a loose tape. Sometimes, the ink refused to function; more often, it was the paper refused to take the ink. The newsprint would arrive on the stands so late the newsboys wouldn't touch them. For all that, the paper sold. Don't ask me how or why. We tried to discover the secret but failed.

When the *Titanic* went down on its maiden trip, I stood by the machine for close on thirty hours without relief. It was Belfast's proud boast that we had built the latest miracle in ships—an 'unsinkable'. The *Titanic* sank on its maiden voyage and carried over twelve hundred souls down with her. But what a scoop it was for the *Echo*!

A murderer named McAfee was to be executed at 8 am on a certain morning. On the previous evening, we had prepared a full account of the murderer's life, his crime and the actual execution itself. We arrived at the news office a few minutes before eight on the morning of the execution. A telephone call came through and we pushed the lever to start the machine. At five minutes past eight, the public were reading a complete report of the execution. That was something like forty-five years ago. Journalism has advanced a lot since those days!

When King Edward VII was dying, we stood by till midnight, three nights in succession, in case His Majesty's death would come through in time to place the news on the streets. On the third night, we were locking up the office when a police constable spoke to us as he passed. "King Edward's dead," he informed us.

Our editor was one of the finest journalists I have ever known. He was rarely seen about the building except in his sober moments, which were rare. But his editorials were classics. Those on 'Temperance' were outstanding. There wasn't a subject under the sun beyond his pen. He was a smoke fiend too, rarely allowing his cigarette to die out. On a certain day, he forgot to light a fresh cigarette, then he died. So did the *Echo*.

I had already cleared out some time before the obsequies.

Meanwhile, I had taken unto myself a wife. I was still quite young and, for that matter, so was the girl I married. Early marriages and large families were the custom. Neither of us realised what lay ahead. Even so, it wouldn't have mattered a tinker's damn. My wages were eighteen shillings a week, so my wife decided to go on working until we managed to collect a home.

She was still working eight years after the wedding and Jim and Joe had been added to the family. It was no life for a young woman. We were soon having to struggle to make ends meet. She was compelled to pay another woman to look after the children while she worked out and I was tied to a low wage without any prospect of leaving the job to search for more remunerative employment. My place would have been filled inside twenty-four hours.

I was becoming very discontented with my work at this time. The intense heat which came from the molten lead and the late hours began to affect my health. I suddenly became obsessed with the idea that I had contracted lead poison. I had met with a number of victims of this dread disease and an unutterable fear gripped me that I, too, would soon come under its terrible ban. Up till now, I had enjoyed perfect health and the very thought of being incapacitated from work drove me nigh frantic with fear. To throw myself onto the labour market in Belfast was to commit mental suicide. We had no savings. Yet to remain at my work would have meant a mental as well as a physical breakdown.

I wrote to my eldest brother, Jim, living in Sunderland, informing him I was going to pay his family a visit. He told me to come and stay as long as I cared. That was all I wanted to know. I left what money I had with my wife, Susan, managed a loan from one of my friends to pay my fare to England and bid goodbye to the printing trade for ever.

Sunderland is a dull English town of shipyards and coalmines. Neither the town itself nor its inhabitants appealed to me. My brother made me welcome but I don't think he approved of me overstaying my welcome. When I broached the subject of getting a start in the shipyards, in which he was a caulker, he was by no means enthusiastic. I stayed on for six weeks in the hope of something turning up, but it was no use and when my brother offered to pay my passage home, I accepted with thanks.

I think he was glad to see the last of me for, at that time, I was a pretty hot-tempered sample of an Ulsterman and, but for his intervention, I would seldom have been out of a scrap. I don't think Englishmen are overfond of

Irishmen in general and Ulstermen in particular. Occasionally, they gave me to understand that most of the Irish troubles were due entirely to the intolerance of Belfast and I gave them to understand that the entire British Navy and Army could never force Ulster to accept anything if we decided to fight it out.

When I arrived back in Belfast, I discovered Susan had given up our little home and gone to live with her parents. I didn't blame her. The few pounds I had left with her couldn't have kept the children and herself more than a few weeks. I was more than ever determined to find a job. The trip across the channel had done me a world of good and cleared my mind of any idea of lead poisoning having got into my system.

I had a notion I might manage to get into the dockers' union. Some of my mates were dockers. During the dock strike, I had given a good lot of time helping the strikers. They were a bit disorganised as a union when I approached the officials. I wasn't too keen about the work. They were a pretty hefty lot of men down at the docks and besides not being used to the work, I wasn't by any means a giant in stature and the loads they were compelled to handle just about scared me stiff.

II

The dock strike in Belfast broke out in June 1907 when I was on the staff of the *Echo*. Discontent had broken out in May because of the conditions at the dockside and the inadequate wages. Jim Larkin, the Dublin leader, had arrived in the city to organise the dockers and carters into one big union. An ultimatum was presented to the shipowners to meet the union representatives, which they immediately rejected.

The dockers' demand was for a sixty-hour week and an increase of wages to twenty-seven and sixpence for ordinary labourers. The companies prepared to resist. They brought over strikebreakers from cross-channel ports as well as a number from Derry and Dublin, housing them on ships anchored in the river. The Scotch, Barrow and Dublin shipping companies agreed to the union's terms, but the Belfast Steamship Company and English railways who ran the Fleetwood and Heyshem steamers, refused to have any dealings with the dockers' leaders.

The Lord Mayor, the Earl of Shaftesbury, immediately called out the military to assist the police in protection of the strikebreakers. Tension in the city rose to a peak. My chum, Ernest Nugent, made a hurried call at my home and called me to the door so that my people couldn't hear the conversation.

"I hear a rumour there's going to be a rumpus down at the docks the night," he told me, full of excitement.

"What's happening?" I asked.

He glanced up the hall to see that all was clear.

"We're going to chase the blacklegs," he explained.

"That'll be a job," I insisted.

"Ach, I don't know," he insisted. "We're gathering separate crowds from the Falls, Shankill and Sandy Row and going to march to the docks."

"But the peelers'll be there," I suggested, "and we might get more than we bargained for."

"Ach, to hell with the peelers!" he exclaimed. "There'll be enough of us to rush them."

"Where'll I see you?" I asked him, having no intention of missing the excitement.

"Sandy Row," he advised me. "That's where the crowd's starting from. They're picking up the Shankill fellows at North Street, then the whole meets at Corporation Square, down at the docks."

"There'll be a hell of a row, Ernie," I suggested.

Nugent nodded his head.

"Let us hope so," he said.

Nugent was that sort of a chap. Didn't give a damn what kind of a row it was so long as he was in it. He was about my age, twenty. Had little education and forgotten the most of what he had been taught. Shortly after the strike, he took on religion, began to study in earnest and was shortly sent out to become a Presbyterian preacher in western Canada. I lost sight of him for some years, then he came over to Belfast on a visit—as a clergyman.

We arrived in Sandy Row that evening around 8 o'clock and found a crowd gathering at the Brewery Buildings. A Union Jack was hoisted above the heads of the crowd and we marched off singing Orange songs. The crowd, which had numbered several hundreds, soon swelled to thousands. I don't believe there was more than a dozen or so dockers amongst us. I saw a couple of plain-clothes policemen mixing with the crowd. They were soon recognised and beat a hasty retreat. The uniformed policemen on beat gave us a wide berth.

We linked up with the Shankill contingent at North Street. By that time, we were an unruly mob. I don't believe we were an asset to the strikers. When we arrived at Corporation Square, facing the docks, we found a double cordon of RIC constables waiting. We swept forward with a rousing cheer. Then the police charged with drawn batons. I didn't notice much after that. I was almost carried along with the retreating crowd.

The police used their batons freely. I lost Nugent in the panic. When I picked him up after the battle, he had lost his cap and half of his coat remained in the hands of a constable.

The carters, who were connected with the dockers' union, made a demand that their wages be increased from twenty-two shillings to twenty-four, but the master carriers absolutely refused to meet the union at any price and the carters threw in their lot with the dockers. The conditions under which the carters laboured were deplorable. They were out at five in the morning getting their horses ready and didn't finish until six that evening—if they were in luck. If their job carried them after 6 pm, it was just too bad. It was their lookout, not the masters.

Later, the coal merchants locked out their employees for refusing an order to leave the union. By July 1st, the strike was in full swing. Lord Shaftesbury placed magistrates around the docks in case their services were needed. There was an ugly atmosphere around the dock side.

Jim Larkin addressed a meeting of 3,000 strikers at the Custom House Steps and threatened "if they want fighting, they'll get their belly full".

A deputation approached the City Council demanding the military be taken off the streets as the city was peaceful. Two Protestant Labour councillors, Alec Boyd and Bob Gageby, spoke on behalf of the deputation and were supported by a number of non-partisan councillors. But Lord Shaftesbury refused to accede to their request.

At a meeting of the strikers in the Exhibition Hall, Councillors Boyd and Gageby, the former a Sandy Row Orangeman, appealed to the men to stand fast.

The press of the city insisted that the strikers' leader, Jim Larkin, who was a Dubliner and a Catholic, had no business in Belfast and should clear out and the strike would end. The following evening, Larkin offered to resign and allow his lieutenant, Councillor Alec Boyd, to become leader. The press immediately dropped their plea for Larkin's resignation. An Orangeman at the head of the strikers would have ruined their attempt to split the strikers into two religious camps.

Ninety per cent of the Belfast Steamship Company's dockers were Orangemen. Many of these men were mates of my own. It was approaching the 12th of July celebrations. It was agreed amongst the strikers that all meetings would be cancelled to allow the Orange demonstrations to be carried out without interference.

The Independent Orangemen supported the strikers and passed a resolution in their support at the field as well as lifting a collection to add to their funds. Alec Boyd was one of the platform speakers. R. Lindsay Crawford, an Imperial Grand Master, and the principle figure on the platform, spoke strongly in favour of the strikers' demands.

Another move was tried. The authorities arrested Larkin for speaking at a political meeting on Harbour property. He refused to give an undertaking to desist, and was fined. The mass of the people backed the dockers, irrespective of creed, and the Joiners' Society, overwhelmingly Protestant, levied three shillings per head of their membership. Willie Walker, their delegate, and other Protestant trade union leaders, took their stand on Jim Larkin's platform. Three of my brothers-in-law were joiners at the time and went all out for the strikers.

It was the first occasion that such an event had happened. A Catholic southerner recognised by his Protestant fellow workers as their champion. It was a dangerous situation for Tory politics. Despite the abuse and one-sided press reports, the men stood firm behind Larkin. There was no sectarian issue although the politicians worked overtime to split the unanimity of the strikers.

Then, the overworked and harassed members of the RIC demanded higher wages and healthier conditions. Constable Barrett, a Catholic, led the mutineers. The Protestant working class of the city had little affection for the Irish constabulary of those days. They were mainly recruited from the Catholic south. The Catholic population swarmed to the support of the constabulary, the Protestants looked on with rising animosity. The stage was set for the sectarian issue.

The strikers took no sides in the police quarrel. They realised that the police revolt would be used against themselves. Disturbances in favour of the police rebels broke out on the Falls and Grosvenor Roads. The military opened fire and killed two young Catholics.

Trade union leaders and Catholic priests spread themselves along the Falls area and managed to quiet the more turbulent spirits. The Unionist Party appealed to the Protestant population to keep calm, which was a fine piece of political graft to separate the unified spirit of the workers that up till now had defied all efforts to drag in a religious background.

Nugent and I were standing at the Protestant end of Albert Street when we heard the gunfire from the direction of the Falls. Nugent caught my arm.

"God, Tommy, I believe that's shooting up the Falls!" he exclaimed in consternation.

I was doubtful. I had never known the police to bring out their rifles during ordinary street riots. It never dawned upon me that the authorities would push matters so far as to order the military to fire on the crowd.

"Who would start shooting up there?" I put to him. "Surely they're not daft enough to start that game and half the town on the side of the dockers!"

He stared at me for a few seconds.

"Do ye know, Tommy, I don't believe the dockers were to hold any meetings the night. That'll be Barrett's supporters kicking up a row with the peelers that's sticking by the masters."

To Ernie, those who opposed the strikers were with the masters.

"Let's go up and see what's going on," he insisted.

I tried to reason with him. I didn't feel like walking into trouble at the time with no particular object in view. However, I gave into him and we walked up towards the Falls. There was a deadly, quiet atmosphere about the streets. Sullen groups of men and women were standing about the corners discussing this dramatic turn of affairs in the strike. One of the women gave us a graphic description of the military opening fire on a defenceless crowd and killing a young man and woman who were mere onlookers.

"That's papishes for ye, the bloody fools!" Nugent exclaimed, as we turned back home. "They bloody well spoil everything. That finishes any chance we had of winning the strike."

The following morning, the Tory papers gloated over the incident with specially printed placards: 'NATIONALIST RIOTS ON THE FALLS—MILITARY ATTACKED'

Constable Barrett was expelled from the police with a few other of the leaders and the mutiny fizzled out. Barrett afterwards rented a public house on the Grosvenor Road, facing the Catholic quarter. At the time, I was living behind Distillery Football Ground in the Protestant area. Some years later, he became a park ranger in Dunville Park in the Falls.

The strikers were eventually forced back on the masters' terms. Neither the carters nor dockers improved their positions. Once the religious issue entered the arena, conditions and wages were relegated to the background and the men mistrusted each other's motives. They still worked their fifty-eight hours and their wages remained as before.

For the time being, the trade union movement in Belfast suffered a setback. The masters had won the first round. Union and non-union workers were to labour together. The dockers' leaders had to accept defeat. Still, for nearly three months the men had battled fiercely against both the masters and the authorities. They had lost the fight but had shown they could stand up to the strain. Hardship, starvation and abuse from press and politician alike did little else but leave bitter memories and the will to carry on the fight in defeat.

The men went back to their work sullen and discontented. Their leaders promised that, in a few years time, with organisation and a stiff upper lip, they would get back their morale and force an issue which, on the next occasion, would be carried through with a more balanced equality of fairness and opportunity.

When the several unions amalgamated to form the Transport and General Workers' Union, running into a million membership, the Belfast district soon discovered their strength and forced their former opponents to concede reform after reform. This wasn't merely a regional union the masters had to face and ignore, but a great organisation that controlled transport on both sides of the channel.

The carters and dockers developed into one of the strongest and best organised unions in Belfast. They became a closed shop. They were the highest paid of semi-skilled workers where they had been the lowest. The strike had shaken the employers as much as the union.

But the sectarian issue which had entered the strike remained. Today, we have two Transport Unions: the Irish Transport Workers' and the Amalgamated Transport and Workers' Union. The one controlled from Dublin, the other from Transport House in London. The Irish Transport members work the foreign ships, the Amalgamated Union the cross-channel shipping. The one membership mainly Catholic, the other overwhelmingly Protestant. It is a tragic situation, but very Irish.

Chapter Seven

'A sight for the Gods'

One of my brothers, Arthur, who was an electric crane driver in the shipyard, spoke to his foreman about me and, in a week's time, I received word that I was to start in the yard in a couple of days, which meant that all the male members of my family would now be employed on shipyard work. Jim was a ship's caulker in Sunderland, Arthur was a craneman in the Belfast shipyard and Wilfred was in the joiners' shop. I was sent out to the construction yards as a plater's helper.

I felt the change in my work doing me good. The breeze blowing in from the open sea was refreshing and clean. I was compelled to rise at 5 am, swallow a bite of food and race a mile and a half to Workman & Clark's shipyard. The helper's wage at that time was twenty-one shillings weekly with, if my recollection is right, a fifty-four hour week. In any case, you started work at 6 am and checked out at 5.30 pm, with two breaks for breakfast and lunch. And no music while you work!

The men whom I now laboured amongst were rough, hardy characters who gambled and drank to their heart's content when money was plentiful, but groused little when bad times came along. They fought and swore and sweated with a carelessness which was exhilarating to me after my closed-in career amongst newsprint machinery. The danger attached to the work didn't seem to affect me in the least, until I received my baptism with the weight of a seven-eight spanner dropping thirty or forty feet into the stokehold and stretching me out for the count.

I was carted to hospital but reported back the following morning to the delight of my comrades. Your first accident was considered a test, the second and third a matter of form.

For the first couple of days, I didn't take too well to the labour, my climbing abilities being a complete fiasco on account of a certain shyness to risk life and limb, and climbing was the one particular talent you were expected to possess as a squad hand.

Our ganger went by the name of Kiltie. Why, I have never been able to discover. He was a small chap, five feet nothing in height, with a deep gash in his upper lip which caused his moustache to take a definite twist upwards. Although somewhat fussy in manner, Kiltie was a decent sort, and we allowed for his shortcomings.

Kiltie had his humorous moments, too. When there would be an unhurried job, he occasionally amused himself and the rest of the squad by giving me a ticklish bit of work to do up the mast or funnel. Watching me crawl round the rim of a fifty-feet high funnel was a sight for the Gods—from the deck. However, those novice days passed and I soon mastered the art of the steeplejack.

There was another grudge the squad had against me. I was a moderate drinker, whilst they, the majority of them at any rate, could lower gallons. But there was one vice they could not teach me—card playing. I was a seasoned gambler and so held their admiration in having a quick eye and brain when the cards were produced.

Perhaps, too, the fact that I had suddenly realised I possessed the gift of versifying their thoughts into the printed word induced the other members of the squad to suffer my utter incapacity of ever learning how to sling a heave of steel plates or erect a temporary staging on my own.

Occasionally, one of the local newspapers would publish a poem above my initials, dealing with the shipyardmen and their work. I boosted the squad in those poems to my heart's content and, in return, they suffered my presence in their midst. So it was without any feeling of inward shame I began with lines of mere doggerel which later—very much later—developed into grammatical verse.

Of all the people whom I have worked amongst—and I have toiled in various grades of manual labour—these shipyardmen were the most thoughtful and kindly, both with their sympathy and practical charity.

Here is one instance of their thoughtfulness. It is inevitable that men receive bodily injuries in such dangerous employment as that of a shipyard, in many cases resulting in death. There were few of us who could not relate some narrow escape from fatality at one time or another.

I don't believe I could name one solitary member of the squad, including myself, who had not been a hospital case.

It was nothing to boast about. There were no medals or decorations attached to the incidents. If the accident laid you out for good, you were carried off and another man took your place in the squad.

But there was something more to it. Your comrades didn't forget you. If you were absent from work, owing to your accident, for more than a fortnight, a couple of your own particular mates held a conference. A 'sheet' was produced in a couple of days and every man on the job was invited to subscribe. The foreman topped the list with the highest amount, then the tradesmen, followed by the labourers. It was carried out quietly, without any fuss or organisation. On the following Saturday, your wife or mother received anything up to five pounds, and the incident was immediately forgotten.

Amongst the squad it was downright bad form ever to refer to it. The fact that you were popular or unpopular never came up.

I had been on the job a couple of months when a serious accident befell Kiltie, which eventually resulted in his death. The squad was shipping boilers aboard at the fitting-out wharf. We were connecting the uptake to the smokeboxes when Kiltie's arm in some way got jammed. Before he could withdraw it, the crane slackened its wires and the full weight of the uptake came down on his forearm. A shout of warning came to the foreman too late. His whistle blew a quick signal and the crane heaved the uptake clear again, but Kiltie's body went limp in our arms.

We got him away to hospital without loss of time. We heard afterwards that septic set in and, in a few weeks time, Kiltie had passed out.

Billie Cullen stepped into Kiltie's shoes as ganger of the squad. Cullen! Every time I think of him, I take a weak turn. A hefty individual, all muscle and brute strength. 'Desperation' we nicknamed him—but not in his hearing—he could use his fists as well as his strength to advantage. He worked twice as hard as any of us, so we didn't mind his bullying methods of getting work done. He had been a stoker on ocean-going vessels, and had travelled round the world several times on tramp steamers. We by no means loved Cullen but we respected him. He was a Catholic, too, while the rest of us were Orangemen.

With the exception of Cullen, the gaffers generally sneered at my poetical efforts. On one or two occasions, when I broke out and tried my hand at prose, they were openly hostile. Perhaps I was too personal regarding gaffers in general. I reckoned them on a parallel with Sergeant-majors, and I detested Sergeant-majors since a lad. Later I even got so far as to publish a volume of poems through the misplaced generosity of a relative of mine in the printing trade, and I have never learned how much he lost in the transaction.

The largest portion of the volume was composed of shipyard verses of a simple nature. The book sold like poison. I was paid off the day it was published and lived in poverty street for nine months. In any case, I was born a few blocks distant from the street, so it didn't hurt.

The public rarely recognises genius in a man at the moment, it takes years for that—sometimes it reaches a hundred years—after his funeral.

Something else happened on the job which had a lot to do with my unfortunate self being consistently named in the future list of 'unwantables'. The foreman was always with us, but it didn't necessarily follow that he should always be the same fellow, which was a pity—for me. The foreman, with whom I had been on good terms, left the shipyard, and another leading hand was promoted to his position. I had never worked under the new foreman—which was more my loss than his. But he had heard about my poetical effusions—and they gave him a sore head.

Few people outside a shipyard can appreciate the glamour which surrounds the building of an ocean liner, or the fascination men have for a particular ship on which they have spent months of hard work preparing for her maiden voyage. Nine hours a day you were part of that ship, toiling in her holds, sweating on one job, having it easy on another, knowing every turn and twist of her alleyways.

She is part of your daily life and, as the day draws near when you must bid her farewell, it seems like parting with something that has held your thoughts and aspirations for, at least, a few months of your industrial life.

A shipyard labourer's pay, previous to the outbreak of the first World War, was twenty-one shillings per week in Belfast and, even with that, you were never sure of a full week's pay because of the possibility of sleeping-in occasionally. Rising at 5 am on a blistering winter's morning was persecution.

When we did manage to shorten the working week, some years later, and bring the starting hour down from 6 am to 8 am, it was a real industrial revolution. When the employers offered a counter proposal to allow the early start to remain and consider the extra hours worked as overtime, the bribe nearly beat us when the men voted upon the two propositions.

It is curious what the offer of higher wages will do to many of those who live by manual labour. Conditions are very often attached to high wages which can easily reduce the worker's status in the social life of a people to that of a beast of burden. Wages can rise and fall according to the fluctuations of trade and industry, but decent industrial conditions, once obtained, are rarely, if ever, tampered with, either by employers or parliament.

It is more important that a manual worker be allowed five or ten minutes to wash his hands before sitting down to his lunch, than he should be paid an extra shilling for 'dirty money'.

When I was employed there, the sanitary arrangements in the Belfast shipyards were primitive in the extreme. A strip of timber attached to a long iron trough accommodated a couple of dozen men without any privacy whatsoever. Not alone that, you were checked in and out. The time allotted—seven minutes.

This is all changed now. Working conditions in the shipyards have improved beyond any worker's expectations. The work is still dangerous and strenuous. Yet my seventeen years labour in the yards have left me many memories of good comradeship and pleasant hours.

Chapter Eight

'A cargo of guns'

I

The Home Rule controversy had died down, or, at least, had been regulated into the background of local politics during my early days in Belfast, but it flared up again shortly after I was married and was the proud possessor of a parliamentary vote. The Home Rule issue was used in every Ulster election to scare the voters into returning a Tory candidate to the Commons. In South Belfast, West and North Down and North Antrim, the Protestant electors turned on the Tories and voted a Liberal or Independent into Westminster.

On the 10th September 1912, Fred Geddis and H.G. Stevenson organised a new movement amongst the young men of Belfast. A meeting was held in the City Hall to form the Young Citizen Volunteers of Ireland. The project was backed by the Lord Mayor and many prominent citizens gathered from all classes and creeds.

The objects of the association were:

(a) To develop a spirit of responsible citizenship and municipal patriotism by means of lectures and discussions on civic matters.

(b) To cultivate, by means of a modified military and police drill, a manly physique, with habits of self-control, self-respect and chivalry.

(c) To assist as an organisation, when called upon, the civil power in the maintenance of the peace.

The movement grew in popularity and, during the course of the next few weeks, seven or eight hundred young men had been enrolled. Politics was banned inside the organisation. The drill instructors were all ex-soldiers. I joined up with the Cliftonville company. Most of the officers were still on the reserve of the regular army. A fife-and-drum and bugle band was formed. We paid for, and were issued out with uniform: silver grey cloth with dark blue facings and silver regimental badges displaying a three-leafed shamrock with the Hand of Ulster embossed on the centre.

We were soon licked into shape, similar to a British territorial infantry battalion of today. Lieut-Colonel Chichester, an Irish Guards reserve officer, took over command, with Major Kerr-Smylie and Captain Harry Mulholland as second and third officers. We made a brave show on our first route march through the city streets. But we carried no firearms, which caused much comment.

The political atmosphere in Belfast during 1912 was growing in intensity. Hundreds of Unionist Clubs were in formation all over Ulster. On April 9th, Sir Edward Carson watched a parade of a hundred thousand men in the Balmoral Show Grounds. It took the force, marching in massed column, three hours to pass the saluting base. On September 28th of the same year, almost half a million Ulstermen signed a solemn league and covenant.

I went along to the City Hall with another Young Citizen, Willie Baxter, who was afterwards killed in France, to sign the Covenant. Baxter was, like myself, a shipyardman, and I am afraid neither of the two of us were keen politicians at the time, but we didn't want to miss any of the fun. Carson arrived with his staff at the City Hall early in the day and was the first to sign. A flag was borne into the chamber supposed to have been carried by the Inniskillen regiment at the Battle of the Boyne. The flag was woven of silk with a crimson five-pointed star in the centre of its Orange folds and the cross of St. George of England in the top left hand corner. No one had ever heard of the existence of this standard previous to the demonstration. It was handed back to its owners and has never been heard of since.

Sir Edward Carson, a southerner, was by this time hailed as the saviour of Ulster and the defender of the Protestant religion. Undoubtedly, he had won the admiration and loyalty of every Ulster Unionist. A small minority had their doubts regarding his sincerity but it did not reduce their hostility to Home Rule.

As the tense atmosphere increased, the Unionist Clubs were disbanded and formed into a new body, the Ulster Volunteer Force, to defend Ulster by force of arms if necessary. The military aspect of this force was soon apparent. Companies, battalions and divisions were organised on an elaborate scale. Ex-NCOs and officers of the regular army were given commands. The men were keen to learn rifle and company drill. There was no need to enforce discipline. It was already an established fact.

Both my brothers, Arthur and Wilfred, were members of the South Belfast Regiment. When there were no service rifles to train the men, dummy guns were used for this purpose rather than waste valuable time once company drill had been mastered. But the men were losing patience with their leaders because of their ludicrous position in playing at soldiers.

The cross channel newspapers were poking fun at the Ulster Volunteers, the nationalists voiced their ridicule.

Baxter and I were invited by one of the instructors to visit a drill hall where the men were being put through their paces. It was a comic-opera sight to watch the men, with stern, determined faces slipping supposed cartridge clips into the magazines of wooden rifles.

Major Fred Crawford was doing his best to smuggle as many rifles into the country as would arm, at least, the border volunteers. But many of the more timid unionists were lukewarm when it came to armed resistance. Crawford went on with his work until the government sat up and considered it time to intervene. Many cases of guns and ammunition were lost in transportation.

The temper of the people had been tested to breaking point on the occasion of Mr. Winston Churchill's visit to Belfast in February, when he addressed a meeting of Home Rulers in the grounds of Celtic Park. The nationalists had rented the Ulster Hall for the meeting but the unionist council managed to gain possession the previous evening and placed a heavy guard in the building and refused to move out. The nationalists were compelled to abandon the meeting in the hall and arrange another meeting place in Celtic Park.

Churchill, who was a member of the Liberal cabinet, arrived in Belfast as the principle speaker at the Celtic Park meeting. His reception, as he and Mrs. Churchill left the Grand Central Hotel to enter their car, was almost a riot. I was employed on the staff of the *Ulster Echo* at the time and was on my way home for luncheon. I noticed the large crowd gathered round the waiting car.

As the Churchills appeared, the crowd surged forward with an angry growl. For a moment, it seemed the car would be thrown bodily over on top of the Liberal leader and his wife. The police, who were trying to humour the crowd up till now, realised the imminent danger and drove into the mob with fists and sticks, holding them off long enough to give the driver sufficient time to start the engine. It was an ugly situation and, but for the driver's quick thoughtfulness in swerving into the first side street, Churchill would never have reached Celtic Park, where a battalion of infantry guarded the approaches in case the unionists of nearby Sandy Row might start trouble in that direction.

As Churchill's car disappeared in the direction of the Falls Road, a strong nationalist quarter, I could hear loud and prolonged cheering further along Royal Avenue, at Castle Place. The angry crowd outside the Grand Central entrance immediately drifted towards that centre of trouble.

When I arrived at the corner of Castle Place, traffic was at a standstill owing to the mass of cheering people who blocked the entire street. From the balcony of the Ulster Club, Sir Edward Carson and his staff were haranguing the crowd with fiery speeches. It was some time before I could battle my way homewards. It had been a day of high tension.

The Young Citizen Volunteers was still an independent body and, because of its contact with the municipality, non-political and non-sectarian. We realised our position was precarious. That sooner or later we too would be swallowed up in the maelstrom of political turmoil. After all, the membership of the corps was overwhelmingly Protestant. I don't suppose there were more than a dozen Catholics, Jews, or Protestant Home Rulers all round.

Besides, Colonel Chichester, our CO, had been appointed officer commanding the East Belfast Regiment of the UVF. We eventually received an emergency order to report to HQ.

II

Some eight hundred volunteers paraded in St. George's Market where Colonel Chichester proposed we join forces with the UVF, threatening to resign on the spot if the majority refused. The vote was practically unanimous and the Young Citizens ceased to be an independent force.

A Special Service brigade had been organised from amongst the rank and file of the UVF members and the Young Citizens were attached to this body because of their standard of training. The Special Service brigade were to be ready for hazardous work if the occasion should arise. By now, most of the UVF were uniformed in khaki, with slouch hats and cavalry bandoliers slung across their shoulders.

Carson inspected the brigade at the Balmoral Show grounds and promised we should be armed and equipped in a few weeks. I noticed my two brothers in the ranks of the South Belfast regiment as the Young Citizens swung through the gates of the show grounds.

The men themselves were settled in regard to the outcome of the whole affair that only force of arms could determine the issue. The politicians and businessmen weren't just as enthusiastic towards this eventuality as the UVF. Their conception of the business was that the Liberal government would drop the Home Rule Bill rather than face a civil war.

But the rank and file trusted Carson. None of us wished to clash with the military or police, yet the spirit of the Volunteers was such that even if a collision with the military was considered inevitable, there was no way out for the service brigade.

Some time later, the Young Citizens had an emergency order delivered at all their homes to parade at Ormiston House, the residence of Colonel Chichester. In pitch dark, we paraded on the lawn facing the house to listen to the Colonel instructing us what to do in the event of a certain plan being put into operation. We dismissed and returned to our various homes knowing we were on the brink of a crisis.

Meanwhile, out at sea, Major Crawford was steaming a cargo of guns and ammunition up and down the coast, waiting his opportunity to run into Donaghadee. In Ulster, the high-ups were wrangling amongst themselves as to the likelihood of a government coup and the consequences to them of such a catastrophe. The rank and file of the UVF were eagerly watching from the shores of Belfast Lough for the signal that was to herald the arrival of the guns.

In Belfast and the surrounding towns, we were standing by, ready and poised for action.

On the evening of Friday 24th April, 1914, messengers on pedal and motor cycles tapped lightly on every Young Citizen Volunteer's home. I was playing with my young son, Jim, when the rat-tat came on my own door. The uniformed figure of one of my YCV sergeants, still astride the saddle of his bicycle, with outstretched arm supporting him against the wall, met me.

"Get into your uniform," he said quickly, "and report at Ormiston House. Make it fast." And he pushed off into the dusk as if shot out of a rocket.

I shouted to Susan to look after the child and hurried upstairs to get into my uniform. To Susan's questions regarding my destination, I returned an evasive answer. Women are damned inquisitive, in any case. I told her I hadn't the foggiest idea what was in the air and couldn't say when I would get back. While I was dressing, she arrived upstairs, with the youngster in her arms, to impress me with her opinion on politics in general and the daftness of certain men who allowed themselves to be led about like sheep by a lot of cranks. I bolted at the first opportunity.

Again, we paraded at Ormiston House in the darkness. We were all keyed up with excitement. It was a beautiful spring night and the slight wisp of wind rustling the overhead branches intensified expectation of mystery and adventure. There was no shouting, usual with military parades. The NCO's collected their sections swiftly, but quietly and without fuss. A cordon of volunteers was placed round the grounds and patrols sent out along the roads to intercept any inquisitive policeman and see what could be done regarding the telephone wires in the neighbourhood. Shortly afterwards, all telephones, in our district, at any rate, were rendered harmless.

Baxter, who was in my section, pinched my arm in the darkness.

"What do ye think of it, Tommy?" he whispered.

We had been warned to keep our voices low.

"We're in it now," I told him.

"What's going on, anyway?" he continued, under his breath.

"How the hell would I know," I hissed. "They didn't tell us a damned thing."

"Who am I supposed to shoot? This magazine of mine's full of live cartridges."

Just with that the butt of his rifle hit my shin and I let out an oath. The sergeant stumbled up to us.

"Will you two fellows keep a bit of quiet. Didn't you hear the orders? No talking." And he slipped back into the darkness.

By midnight, we noticed the usual stillness which pervades country roads was being shattered with the heavy rumble of lorries and lighter tread of private cars. Few of these used their horns. In the early hours, word was passed along to be ready. A motor cyclist swung past us through the gates of Ormiston. A lorry loomed out of the darkness and the driver sang out a greeting as he turned the vehicle into the carriage way.

The tarpaulin was stripped from the lorry in a few seconds and rifles and ammunition were soon being transferred to the cellars. Our patrols were now holding up everybody who could not be identified and turning them back. We had every approach to the house under surveillance. Luckily, there were no incidents. If military or police had arrived on the scene, it would have been just too bad. Some of us would probably have lost our lives.

It isn't my intention to write a detailed account of the organisation of the gun-running exploit, the names of those responsible, nor the manner in which it was carried to a successful conclusion. I was a mere unit in the organisation, a private of the Young Citizen Volunteers. But it was certainly an extraordinary achievement. Not a shot was fired.

III

In brief, this is a short sketch of what happened during the night. A battalion of the UVF marched to the dockside and lined up facing one of the empty berths, just as dusk fell. Police and custom men hurried to the scene. They waited patiently for hours. Not a damned word was exchanged between the government men and the volunteers. They were both waiting for something to happen. It did. Well into the night a coaster steamed up the river and drew alongside the dock.

Tension! The police covered the custom men as they boarded the ship. The UVF stood grimly by, making no movement to interfere. The ship was searched. Not even a popgun was unearthed.. The custom came down the gangway, spoke to the police, and moved off home. The police lingered for some time, then followed. There were a few brief commands and the UVF marched away—left, right, left, right—the dockside resumed its drab, gloomy night shape.

Meanwhile—a tramp steamer, the *Mountjoy*, steamed into Larne harbour with a cargo of 340 tonnes of rifles and ammunition. The police barracks and coastguard station were surrounded by UVF men. Not a man was allowed to pass through the cordon. Hundreds of volunteers were unloading the shipment of arms. Heavy and light motors were loaded up and disappeared into the darkness. A couple of steamers drew alongside the *Mountjoy*, trans-shipped part of the cargo, and glided away towards Bangor and Donaghadee. The police and custom men in these ports were also sealed off.

Six hundred motor vehicles were speeding in every direction along the roads of counties Down and Antrim, loaded with arms and ammunition. Arriving at their destination, a crowd of silent, grim-faced men would suddenly appear out of the darkness, unload the material, and fade as silently into the darkness again. The lorry would swing round and speed off on another errand.

The following day was Saturday. By the time the operation had concluded, those of us who were manual workers found it impossible to check in on our jobs. I was a plater's helper in the shipyard, so forfeited a day's pay. So did the majority of my comrades. On dismissal, I proceeded home to catch a few hours sleep before Susan would commence her inquisition.

The news of the gun-running spread like wildfire through Ulster. Every town and village was celebrating the event. What the government intended to do about the affair didn't worry us much. The dummy rifles were pitched into the furnaces. In every hall, hut and arms dump, we were slapping the magazines of the rifles with affection. A new spirit was abroad. We felt pretty sure of ourselves now.

Sentries were posted at every arms dump in the province. In case of sudden raids on the arsenals, we had dispatch riders ready to spread the alarm that would bring thousands of volunteers to the spot in less than an hour. We were elated and ready for any emergency. Our women were neither alarmed nor enthusiastic. I don't believe they were terribly worried on our account either. The girls in the warerooms enjoyed the excitement and added extra pastry to their morning cup of tea just to celebrate.

Some five hundred thousand Ulster men and women had signed a Solemn League and Covenant on the 12th September 1912, declaring they would stand together in defence of Ulster against Home Rule. Previous to that date, we were against Home Rule for any part of Ireland. How or why our leaders had changed their attitude to a stand for Ulster alone, we neither questioned nor understood. Possibly, it was a safer and more logical defence.

Now we had sufficient guns and equipment to make a fight, there was no turning back. The men were too determined to carry the issue through for our leaders to even think of a future retrenchment. The organisation was nigh perfect in training and morale was high. In fact, many of us were eager to prove our ability to face the British government forces, or the Irish National Volunteers who were now recruiting in the south.

It wasn't long until the British government went into action. Warships anchored off Larne, and a destroyer flotilla sailed up the Lagan to dock at Belfast. They were welcomed and entertained by the Lord Mayor officially. We were by no means scared. I think we enjoyed the situation.

Some time in May or June, the UVF Council decided to stage a public demonstration of their strength. The Young Citizen battalion, being the most advanced in military training, was ordered out on a route march through the central thoroughfares of the city. We were to parade fully armed with rifles and bayonets, as well as a machine gun detachment. The city was full of rumours on the morning of the route march. There were whispers that operations on a warlike scale would commence that day. But the authorities merely stood by.

Headed by Colonel Chichester and Major Kerr-Smylie, mounted on chargers, and led by our regimental band, we made a brave show in our silver grey uniforms and rifles and bayonets glinting in the hot sun of a summer's day. Bringing up the rear, guarded by a strong escort, was a brace of machine guns mounted on tripods and bogies.

A dense mass of citizens crowded the city centre to greet us with cheers and hat waving and, as we swung along High Street, one was apt to remember such another demonstration in the same thoroughfare, one hundred and twenty years earlier, when the old Irish Volunteers demonstrated their defiance of the English government of the day and their sympathy with the French people in the taking of the Bastille.

Then came the rumours of war. Europe was tense with expectancy. The British people's minds went off the Ulster question and concentrated on, to them, more important matters. We, on the other hand, were still self-interested on our own affairs. Then the Germans invaded Belgium and set Europe aflame. Local issues became unimportant in the welter of world politics.

Although the Home Rule crisis passed off without the clash between the Crown Forces and the UVF as expected, you may take my word for it, if such a catastrophe had occurred, the rank and file of the movement would have fought it out. They were ready and willing to shed blood for the cause, their own or that of anyone else, so long as Ulster remained in the United Kingdom.

There was nothing comic regarding their determination to resist. They would have martyred themselves wilfully and recklessly. One shot fired would certainly have set Ulster ablaze. They allowed Carson to lead them, but he could not have held them back. Even to this day, I look upon the outbreak of the 1914 struggle as a coincidence which saved the country from a bloody civil war.

Chapter Nine

'Workers—a yearning for expression'

I

A pay-off in the shipyard is an unpleasant occurrence in the life of any shipyardman. But it is inevitable and, from the manager down to the smallest catch-boy, it is a procedure attended with many regrets.

With the new pay-off came the rumour that Workman & Clark's

shipyard was closing down for all time. For years, our local yards had smashed the international shipbuilding records of the world with ease and assurance. No foreign liner was so big we could not eclipse it in size; no beauty or design so great that we could not fashion a more gorgeous example; no cargo ship, mail boat or liner with a Belfast-built stamp on the maker's name plate but brought fame and commerce to the city's port. The expansion and importance of the city had been built round its shipyards.

Like a blast from a furnace mouth came the post-war slump, bringing in its wake the stagnation of the shipbuilding industry. The Belfast yards held grimly to their well-deserved prominence through the first troubled years of the slump, but finally they too had to slacken down owing to meagre orders and dwindling trade. Then came the final catastrophe of the *Bermuda*. Costing millions of pounds and over a year's toil of the finest craftsmen in the world, it was snuffed out of existence by scorching flames in the space of a few hours.

If I could only express in words the misery that one feels when the beauty created by his and others' hands through months of labour and sweat is blasted in a solitary night from being a symbol of man's ingenuity into a smouldering heap of ruins!

And this was to be our Waterloo! There was a despondent feeling amongst the boys. A sort of gloominess they had never experienced in any of the numerous pay-offs which had occurred at various periods of shipyard depression. There were none of the usual jocular remarks as to where we would spend the forthcoming holidays. We realised that this was our last ship and our last day in the shipyard for many months, perhaps years. The optimists, and we had our full complement of them, were silent. A great shipyard was on the point of closing down.

And what a finish! Perhaps the weather was concerned in the plot. The rain fell in proverbial cat-and-dog fashion as we made our way along the quayside. It beat in our faces, trickled off our caps down the backs of our necks, ran down our overcoats into our boots, leaving nothing dry but our throats. We lifted our time-boards at the gatehouse and hurried on.

It was breaking dawn. A wet, misty, miserable dawn. The devil's own way of heralding a great catastrophe. I tripped over an angle bar in the dusk and floundered into a miniature lake, splashing my comrades in a shower of mud. My mate cursed sourly and told me to watch my step. Another time he would have laughed heartily.

We halted a moment under cover to shake the raindrops off our caps. The panorama of what had recently been a shipyard lay before us. The long avenues of tall staging poles stood like sentinels. How the worker manages to hide his real feelings has always been a mystery to me—and I am one of them myself. In the early morning, we were despondent; during the day, too busy to think; the last hour, hilarious.

"What's this for?" asked one chap, as he was handed his pay docket by the foreman. "Free meals?"

"Probably," retorted the foreman, without humour, "it's going to pay for your last meal." We all roared at the foreman's sally.

"I wonder," remarked another, "if the other yard's short of hands?"

"Short of hands!" snorted my mate. "They'd need an extension if they take us on."

So the chaff flew.

We packed our tools away and locked the boxes. One of the wisecracks wrote 'Wanted' in chalk across his boxlid. When he looked round again, someone had added 'in 1957'.

An ominous silence was now creeping over the ship. Hammers had ceased to ring; caulking tools were silent. No hum of the drill. No life. An oil tanker isn't the cheeriest of ships at any time.

We lit our pipes as we took the road to the time-office to lift our lying-time. The boys all seemed happy. Not a worry. Devil a thought of tomorrow. The manager passed us on the road. He, too, was smoking. In working hours too! Christopher Columbus!

In a few moments, we had ceased to be employed workmen. The squad separated for their different homes. "So long!" "See you again." "What about a drink?" "Mind the wife don't nag you."

The next morning, at the Labour Exchange, we scowled at one another. You don't need to pass bills in parliament to squeeze these men off the unemployment fund. They'd eat dirt out of your hand to get off it themselves.

I was writing feverishly now. Poems and articles under my name were appearing pretty frequently in the Belfast and Dublin newspapers. But I couldn't keep pace with the bread-and-butter problem. I had four boys now, Samuel being born whilst I was serving with the Ulster Special Constabulary. I was receiving something like twenty-seven shillings a week unemployment benefit for my wife and three children, with a 'gap' every alternative five weeks. This meant, every five weeks you received nothing. The baker, the grocer, and rent man went unpaid. It was a horrible system. And there was no escape. The thing was wearing me down.

II

At last, I met with final disaster. I was ordered to appear at the 'Glass House' one morning when I held out my hand for the usual benefit. The 'Glass House' was the torture chamber of the Labour Exchange. Here you were examined regarding your attempts to seek work. There was never any question about the officials offering you work. There wasn't any in the city, or out of it, they could offer you. But they had to reduce the 'Live Register' somehow, so they insisted you seek something which didn't exist. I think my doom was sealed before I even entered the room. Still, they went through the formality of cross-examination. "Where were you on such a date?" "Who did you apply to?" "What time would that be?" "Have you ever tried this firm?" "No! Why not?" "You may go now."

I still remember the crucifixion, and it leaves a bad taste in my mouth. The result of my case was handed to me a few days later. I was to receive a further two weeks benefit then my unemployment insurance was finished. I was at a dead end. What was I to do? How was I to live? What about my wife, my boys, my home?

One of my friends came to my rescue. He suggested I use my typewriter to advantage. Why not get the loan of a duplicating machine and start a typewriting agency? He would cover the rent of a suitable office for six months. I accepted the offer and actually had the audacity to sign off the Bureau before I received my final payment. The Bureau official suggested I sign on the Health Insurance. He thought I was really ill.

I turned my back on the Labour Exchange in a depressed state of mind. The effect of contact is sufficient to cause that depression. I cursed the damned place, and began to whistle a jazz melody. Why should I be depressed? I had health and strength, a fully developed mind, with an unlimited capacity of reasoning powers. There were thousands in the city, blind, maimed, incurable souls who would gladly exchange places with me irrespective of wealth or the position they may have held.

Why should I grieve? Were not the stars that spangled the night with beauty and mystery as much mine as anyone else's? Hadn't God painted the landscape with gorgeous colours so that I might feast my eyes on the Creator's handiwork and feel all this was made for my happiness? It was much easier to live one's life in a world in which one had no labour in the making.

To lift one's self up from the occupation of a shipyard worker to that of a business man on a small scale takes some doing. Possibly without assistance it would be a difficult undertaking. My opinion, as a wage-earner, regarding all business men, was that they were grasping capitalists, whether in a big or small way, whose sole aim in life was to fleece the poor hard-working wage-earner. I confess that my opinions have changed somewhat from the days I occupied that little office in Donegall Street.

I had my business card and, as some people prefer high sounding phrases, my up-town address, but precious little else. My five pounds soon vanished into as many shillings but my reasoning powers increased tenfold and my narrow outlook in politics, which was fiercely socialistic in theory, went through a broadening-out process.

As a wage-earner, I had no worries concerning income. The responsibility was upon my employer and I was protected by certain legal rights. Out of employment, I could always fall back upon insurance benefit. Now, as a business man, I had to fall back on my own reserves—which were nil.

True, if I felt inclined, I may have remained in bed another hour but my clients didn't seem over anxious to knock at my office door twice.

I used to envy the man of business, not because of what he had, but because of what I had not. Like the rest of my comrades of the workshop, it was my dream to be self-supporting, to be independent. I have attained both these aspiring heights; my ambitions have been gratified; but my dreams vanished along with the remains of the five pounds.

Yet I do not regret my advent into the world of one-man business. I ceased to be a burden on the state for a year at least and felt a certain amount of satisfaction in knowing there was still enough fight left in me which the 'dole' had not been able completely to crush. And round me, in the neighbouring offices, were a number of stout fellows—a tailor, a poster-writer, a trader's agent—whose optimism and sympathy I not alone valued, but still respect.

During that year as a typewriting expert, I was at my wits' end in my efforts to hold my self-respect as well as my sense of humour, which had, up till now, never deserted me. My best week brought me in twenty-five shillings, my worst—there wasn't any worst, they were all bad.

I advertised to type plays, poems, stories, any cursed thing needing typing at a shilling a thousand words, and I was so weak from undernourishment, my limited speed was about four thousand words a day. God, but I suffered agonies during that year which I had to remember and family worries nearly drove me over the brink.

Then, one afternoon, Ruddick Millar, who was reporting for the *Irish News*, a few doors further up the street, called at my office and invited me to accompany him to a discussion on drama which was to be held in the YMCA.

The late Richard Rowley, a linen merchant and poet, was the lecturer and, when he had finished a rather brilliant discourse on Irish drama, a discussion was opened. I had never taken part in a public discussion in my life, but here was a subject I could speak on, and I did. Afterwards, Richard Rowley had a long talk with me, insisting that I should try my hand at playwriting. I had never been backstage in my life. I had read plays, sure enough, but with what understanding? True, I had been a first-nighter since I was a child, if I could manage to beg, borrow or steal the gallery fee. I promised Richard Rowley I would try. The following day, I started on a shipyard play—*Workers*.

After four months steady work, I offered it to Richard Rowley. He was pleased with the effort and handed it over to the Northern Drama League, of which he was then president. The Drama League sent the script back to me with the excuse they found it impossible to gather up enough dialect speakers to put it across. The Rosario Players, who excelled at George Shiels' plays, admitted it was too revolutionary. The Ulster Theatre accepted the play and offered seven per cent royalties, which I accepted with delight.

I went crazy with joy. At last I had succeeded. All my ambitions, all my dreams had come true! The Ulster Theatre cast the play and put it into rehearsal. Then I received a letter of regret from them to say the manager of the Opera House had rejected permission to include my play in their repertoire because of its working-class tendencies.

I was licked. I had made my effort and failed. The years of misery and poverty were to go on. I was no weakling at taking it on the jaw. All my life, I had got it there, but I had made the supreme effort of my life and it had come to nothing. It was only a play, possibly a third-rate attempt at that, but I had put everything I knew into it. I had drawn the characters from real life and the dialogue was their everyday speech. If I had failed to give a true picture of life, then my own life was an illusion. I knew I should never write again. Faith in myself had passed out. Yet I realised in my heart, whilst I lived in the everyday drama which went on around me, that I could never hope to blind my senses to a yearning for expression.

Chapter Ten

'A burst of applause'

I

Meanwhile, there came a split in the ranks of the Ulster Literary Theatre. Richard Hayward, J.R. Mageean, and several other members broke away and formed the Belfast Repertory Theatre. Hayward offered to give *Workers* a show at the first opportunity, reducing the royalties down to five per cent, and retaining the full dramatic rights to himself. I would have taken one per cent had he offered it. I was at my wits' end to make a shilling or two, and I didn't care where it came from, who supplied it, or why. My whole family wanted something to eat.

Then came the announcement that *Workers* would be produced at the famous Abbey Theatre by Hayward's company, on the 13th October 1932. Next to being buried in Westminster Abbey, most Irish playwrights yearned for their play to be produced in the Abbey Theatre. Sure enough, it caused the sensation Hayward wished for. He believed if we could only manage an audience the play would do the rest. The weeks between were agony for me. I haunted the rehearsal rooms and Sunday papers haunted my office.

My new play was boosted all over the Sunday papers. I have to admit, even today, those Sunday reporters practically made me an audience. I wondered could my play hold them?

The initial performance of a playwright's first attempt is an experience of mental excitement not everyone would care to go through. The pleasurable anticipation of seeing one's effort staged in a public theatre, especially when that particular theatre has earned an international fame, and the author happens to be an unemployed shipyardman, is an episode in a man's life that mere words are incapable of recording.

The two nights previous to the play were purgatory to me. Sleep was out of the question. Not that failure could mean any material change in my life, for there is no stage below labouring for a livelihood—except starvation. But success meant an upward climb; the first rung of the ladder.

On the evening of the production, I went up to the dressing-rooms to wish the players good luck. The most of them were old-timers at the game, yet a first production has a similar effect on the actor as it has on the author. The entire company was suffering from nerves.

For the first time in my life, I viewed a performance from a comfortable seat in the stalls. The Gods had lost an habitué. Afterwards, I was informed I sat with a very select company composed of a number of Irish nobility, a Chief Justice, members of the Dáil and not a few prominent figures representing the social life of Dublin. Thank goodness I was innocent of the fact.

The curtain went up and I saw the characters I had conjured in my brainbox come to life. I admit they were strange to me, so unlike the mental picture were they. Their speech and actions were those of ordinary humans.

The action of the play seemed to drag during the first act. The audience was being bored. I could feel it in my bones. I felt like sobbing out in self-pity. The conceit went clean out of my being and I felt small and foolish and wished to Heaven I never written the thing.

When the curtain dropped on the first act, there was a slight ripple of applause—sympathy for the author probably. I took side-long peeps at the audience to treasure the memory—in case it might only be a memory.

I was in my place when the curtain went up for the second act. The setting was perfect—but it was the producer's, not mine. The audience became interested. Soon they began to laugh heartily at the humorous situations, to subside quickly when the play took a dramatic turn. It was a public house scene, and it was one thing I knew something about. I became interested in my own play—an unforgivable sin, I believe. At the conclusion of the act, there was a burst of applause, and I knew I was winning.

An unholy joy took possession of me. Years of poverty, misery, disappointment, were forgotten in that solitary moment of Heaven. Four times the curtain rose and fell before the word 'author' was mentioned. Someone touched me on the shoulder and whispered, "Go ahead, lad, you've deserved it".

I managed to get round to the stage somehow, my heart bursting and tears running down my cheeks. The tremendous welcome I received struck me dumb with astonishment. I stammered out some words of thanks to the company and the audience, which seemed to satisfy both parties. And so I, an unemployed shipyardman, became a playwright. Just a week previous I had been elected Worshipful Master of Sandy Row True Blues, Independent Orange Lodge. What an announcement that would have been from a Dublin stage!

The Belfast Repertory Company returned to their home town without the author of their play. I lingered on in the neighbourhood of the Abbey for another twenty-four hours. It was *my* hour.

Even if I were to write successful plays to the end of my life, I will never be able to live that hour over again. It had been many years since I had last been in Dublin, and this was my first visit to the Abbey. The theatre had a peculiar fascination for me. The fact that it was the national expression of Irish dramatic art stirred me to the core.

And they were a grand audience. Against my strongest principle, I rose with them during the playing of 'The Soldier's Song'. I have to admit I was humming 'The Boyne Water' into myself as a sort of repudiation.

I met poor Tom Casement on my first trip and he and I became fast friends. We were in the foyer of the theatre, one morning, when the late W.B. Yeats entered. Casement brought us together. Yeats looked me over curiously and asked me if I had ever offered a script to the Abbey. When I said "No", he bade me "Good Morning" and went on his way.

Back in Belfast, *Workers* packed the Empire Theatre for a week. Although it was played before a variety audience they gave my play a tumultuous welcome. My shipyard comrades swamped the Gods at every performance, and I can still hear their cheers of encouragement in my ears to this day. They were great pals.

I paid off a few debts, and went back to my typewriting agency. Inside a fortnight, I was back where I started. But this time I didn't worry. One of my dreams had come true, I had been given a chance. What more could a man ask for! It was up to me to keep going. And I did.

The Quota Press offered to publish a collection of my poems and I immediately started on the book. Within a few months I had *Songs of an Out-of-Work* ready for publication. The critics gave the volume a sympathetic reception, but poetry doesn't sell in Ulster. My first publication, *Songs from the Shipyards*, published in 1924, had passed into oblivion.

Meanwhile, I was being invited to lecture to various societies in Ulster. A few paid my expenses—and something. It was good fun, for I got a lot of stuff off my chest I had been wanting to say for ages. Curiously enough, no socialist or labour group ever showed the least interest in either myself or my plays, although all my life I had striven, by voice and pen, to encourage my fellows to seek better conditions and live for the betterment of mankind. Perhaps it was because I wouldn't touch politics my socialist friends found little to interest them in my work.

Any encouragement I received came from the middle classes and my shipyard pals. The Common Room Staff of Queen's University invited me as a guest to dinner in company with Forrest Reid and Richard Rowley, a gesture which I still appreciate.

One of our provincial colleges asked me to come down and lecture to the pupils. The Principal invited me to have dinner with him before the meeting. I hadn't sat down to a decent dinner for donkey's years, and I wasn't quite sure whether knives and forks were still in use. I tried to dodge the dinner but I failed. The Principal's sister sat with us. I got through three courses without incident. The fourth was dessert. It was some rainbow coloured stuff which made my eyes pop twice. But times had changed since my dinner days and so had the utensils in which it was served. The trifle was brought in, dancing about in a large-sized glass.

"Are you fond of this?" the Principal's sister asked me.

I'm sure there was poetry in my eyes as I answered, "Yes."

She handed me the glass and I was fully half way through with it before I realised the blasted thing was between three of us. My heart sank, but I kept my head, and finished the entire lot without blinking an eyebrow. Not a word was spoken during the final act, but I noticed the maid's hands shook. I felt pretty sick, too. But it couldn't be helped.

I lectured to that particular college quite a number of years afterwards—but there were no more dinners.

Two of my boys were working now: Jim at the printing and Joe, who had gone to the farming in Canada, left it inside a week, tramped his way back to Montreal, stowed away on a Belfast ship and returned home within the year, and was now working with construction engineers. He was barely seventeen. Noel and Sam were still at school. They were great lads, all of them, but they were having a pretty rotten deal out of life.

Hayward asked me for another play and I started on *Machinery*, finishing the last act at the end of three months. Jimmie Mageean, Hayward's producer, liked the new play, and it was put into rehearsal. I had much to thank Mageean for, not alone that he produced every one of my plays, but for the patience he took with my want of stage knowledge.

Traitors followed, which had been inspired by the Outdoor Relief riots during 1932. Then *Castlereagh*, an historical play of the '98 rebellion which, I suppose, was my supreme effort at playwriting. A few months previous to *Traitors* being produced, I got work with Belfast Corporation. Was it a relief! Honestly, a few more years in that office in Donegall Street and I certainly would have finished in a mental hospital. Play-writing had saved my life.

I was now bordering on the fifty mark, with a wife and four boys to look after. Joe had taken the wanderlust again and went off to sea. He was somewhere along the East African coast on a tramp steamer. Noel had started work and there was only Sam to worry about. I was feeling rightly pleased with myself.

Then the 1935 riots commenced. We all thought we were in for a repetition of 'The Troubles'. On this occasion, there were only seven or eight deaths from shooting before the Constabulary managed to sweep the trouble makers off the streets. Jim happened to be working in a Catholic quarter at the time and a few gunmen arrived at his place of business, ordering him to clear out at the point of the gun. He was given five minutes to leave the premises and did the job in five seconds. He had never been much of a politician up till then. In three week's time, he was an Orangeman.

During the 1935 riots, the authorities studied a new technique in quelling the disturbance. Instead of placing a cordon of police between the opposing crowds, they erected a corrugated iron partition between the opposing districts, so that neither side could see what was going on in the opposite camp. It worked, except in one instance.

The back entrance of Clifton Street Orange Hall was situated in Regent Street, a Catholic quarter. When the authorities erected the barricade between Regent Street and Hanover Street, which was predominantly Protestant, they closed the Orange Hall entrance into Regent Street. There was an unholy row when the Orangemen discovered what had happened and a deputation immediately made tracks to the police to have the mistake remedied.

To demolish the Hanover Street barricade would be heading for trouble. After a conference, it was decided to allow the Hanover Street barricade to remain, and build a further partition lower down Regent Street, thus enclosing the Orange Hall in a little recess of its own. Once, when Richard Rowley and I were passing through on a dark winter's eve, we discovered that courting couples were making quite a rendezvous of the place.

Chapter Eleven

Epilogue

The end of hostilities found Mary and I in a flat above Charles Haig's photographic studio at Royal Avenue. My old home, in the Shankill district, still bore signs of its battle scars.

The effect of the war on the Carnduff clan was similar to the records of many other families. The war had finished our home life. Joe had returned from his four years in a prisoner-of-war camp, three stones lighter in weight, bade the sea a long farewell, married a Belfast girl and settled down in the city.

Noel had married an English girl living at his home port during his service with the navy, and decided to live in Sheerness after his demob. Jim applied for a post with Wix Brothers of Johannesburg, was interviewed and sailed for South Africa in 1947, his wife and two boys following him out shortly afterwards.

Samuel applied to the Australian government for an assisted passage, was accepted as an immigrant, and sailed for South Australia in 1949. That completed the dispersal.

What boys they were! To each other they were mean and generous, antagonistic and sympathetic, surly and cheerful; they would share their last bite and also pinch each other's share of what was going; they fought each other like cats and dogs, but were steadfastly loyal if trouble came upon any one of them. If they arrived home at an unearthly hour, I never inquired as to the cause. They generally told me. When they didn't, I wasn't worried. They were as bit a lot of devils as the worst of them, and as good a bunch of lads as the best.

When I was badly off, so were they. If I had dry bread for breakfast, they didn't fare any better. If I could spare them a few coppers for the cinema, I gave them all I had. If I had no money, no cinema. How they grew up into decent intelligent men through my rearing, I don't know. But they did. I suppose they had guts.

In the winter of 1946, I was transferred from the Civil Defence to my old job in the Belfast Corporation Surveyor's Department, as a yardman. I had passed the sixty mark and my muscles lost the flexibility of the fifties, although I still felt fit and full of vim. But my staying powers had deteriorated, and I wasn't what I had been, if the reader understands.

To be kicked in the pants occasionally doesn't do one the least bit of harm. Nor to be half-drowned in the backwash of life isn't any disgrace. So long as you don't pull any other beggar down with you, you've a chance of survival. It's having a traveller beside you when you come up for the third time that drags you under again. Alone, you can grab something and pull yourself out of the murky waters and start life afresh.

To be financially safe may bring you a fine house, plenty of food, as much amusement as one could wish for, and a host of friends. That would spell comfort. But if you should lose all these things—you have nothing left.

Financially, I have been in the woods all my life. I've never had a fine house, my food has been plain and my friends few. In contrast, I have a good home, although I could do with a bath and a garden. The food Mary cooks is wholesome and rarely tinned. Whatever friendships I have contracted have developed through similar tastes or mutual sympathies, never because of financial benefits. These things may not affect one's comfort, but they do one's contentment.

I am fond of horses and dogs, but I prefer human beings as companions. The song of the lark and the thrush holds me spellbound. So do the voices of the choir at St. Anne's Cathedral. When I visit the Botanical Gardens in Belfast, I never fail to enthuse on the brilliant colourings of gorgeous hothouse and tropical flowers. Yet, when I roam the wild moorland behind the hills overlooking Belfast I go crazy with joy as I scramble along the beaten tracks between acres of purple heather, wild bracken, and the golden sheen of the whinbush.

At home I read the evening and daily newspapers. Anti-partition, strikes, murders, hold-ups, earthquakes, Iron Curtains, revolutions, and divorces, well-boiled and served with appetising sauces. It would be a stinking, rotten world if one were to read only and not think. The ordinary decent little things that men and women do in their everyday lives are not recorded as news. You have to take note of them yourself without searching the newspapers for reports.

Even with all these catastrophes happening every minute of the day, there are wonderful occurrences taking place in the normal course of events. Winter will pass and spring and summer arrive. Trees will survive the autumn and winter and spring to life again. Flowers will bud and bloom whether the United Nations functions or collapses. There will be a sunrise and sunset, and the mood and stars will shed their radiance, long after wars, famines, and revolutions have disappeared from the earth.

If the politician, both north and south, would pipe down for a space and let the people alone, it would do Ireland a world of good. Actually, none of us worry a great deal about politics until we are goaded into howling at each other. The most of us haven't the faintest idea why we lose our tempers. We have so many problems of our own to face we could do with a break. It's a good job the horses and cattle and poultry have no political sense. If they had, we'd be sunk.

Meanwhile, I'll carry on the way I've been doing at present, barring by a stroke of fortune's wheel, I slip into a bundle of money. In that case, I would be interested in building a little theatre for Belfast. I could spend the evenings encouraging young fellow artists, actors, painters, poets and singers, to add a little more enthusiasm for the arts in the hearts of my own Ulster folk.

If the reader doesn't hear from me again, it is because it should never have been written. That what I have seen and heard and participated in was of small matter in a world of various interests.

Then I shall go on labouring till I am sixty-five, apply for my pension, retire to some small nook in a public park, gossip and play dominoes with other pensioners—and, in the course of a few years, fade out and be forgotten by my fellows.

Other Writings

Belfast is an Irish City

It is generally felt, by those who share in what we are vaguely termed 'cultural movements' in Belfast, that they extend much livelier goodwill towards similar work in other parts of Ireland than they enjoy in return. There are many explanations for what I call 'the national attitude' towards Belfast, but the fact is that it is taken for granted by the south that anything emanating from Belfast must be bigotedly Protestant, hostile and antinational. This should be little surprise to us here in Belfast itself where Roman Catholic students attending the university are directed to take no part in College societies, for it is the people who hold such views or those who subscribe to them or are shaped by them who have the ear of the south.

And yet Dublin is in the minds of all of us who write books or plays, or paint; in a vague sort of way, it is our capital city. I remember my own feeling that I had really got to the heart of things when I found myself in the Abbey watching a play of mine come to life on stage; though I had been Worshipful Master of an Orange Lodge in my day. I still have that feeling about Dublin despite the fact that, in the meantime, I have often felt the south has turned its back on us, and has forced us in on ourselves so much that we have begun to look on Belfast as a sort of city state; almost a fatherland. Many things happen which make us think that the south is not adult-minded enough to accommodate people of our freedom of thought within a united Ireland. Perhaps if we were patriots we should be prepared to risk some hardship and unfairness and trust to the future for the remedy, but then we are not patriots. We are merely Irishmen.

And as I am an Irishman, so are the others of my kind up here in Belfast, and I am a Sandy Row-born Protestant, who passed through all the normal organisations of my kind, including membership of the Special Constabulary. Our advice to the Roman Catholic politicians in the north, who are so insistent that they speak for the nationalists, would be to go out on to the highways and byways of Ireland and paint on all the dead walls a truth that is yet hidden from the people. That Belfast is an Irish city: that the Protestants of Belfast are as Irish as the Catholics. The shock might help the nationalists, north and south, to grow up and realise that the country has a minority problem, which is religious not racial in character, however much British interference in the matter has made it an issue between the two countries.

This wakening up would reflect itself early in a few simple changes in popular behaviour. For example: Is there any adult-minded nation which opens its football matches with a sectarian hymn? Is there any nation which, in a public ceremony of a national character, does anything corresponding with the practice of saying the Rosary at Easter ceremonies? Let there be prayers for the dead by all means at religious ceremonies on such occasions, church parades of all denominations, but surely the public ceremony should be open to all creeds or no creeds.

Again the question of the Gaelic League. Now very few of us take much interest in Gaelic tradition which is, after all, a hangover of the country fireside tales which have not much place in our folklore. We would be quite pleased to learn that those who are interested in the language are making headway. Many of us even would encourage our children or grandchildren to learn it, and we would gladly see them off to Donegal for a holiday among the Gaelic speakers. But we do not wish that our children would have to acquire their education through Gaelic and we are afraid that might happen to them in a united Ireland. But nobody ever tries to get in touch with us on this matter.

In pointing out these worries and the other signs of the complete lack of consciousness of a minority problem in the nationalist, I am not suggesting that the Protestants of Ireland have been reactionaries on the main question of the day, political independence. What I am suggesting, however, is that this reactionary rôle is not due to any doubt in ourselves that we are Irish. Nor do I believe that sectarian strife would have taken such a hold if it had not been incited from high places, but the incitement has been there and the counter-measures have been very weak indeed. Even at that, it is an open question whether the sectarian strife in Belfast is worse than what breaks out now and then in many, but it is more played on by the politicians of both sides.

Strangely enough, my impatience with sectarian strife in Belfast is not that it delays national unity. That will come one day, but I would rather be as I am meanwhile. My moan is that it delays the mental and spiritual growth of the city. The mind is intimidated and confused by it and, worse than all, it spreads a feeling that the people are powerless before it and cannot dominate their circumstances. This develops a kind of tribal mind in people and, when misfortune hits, all they can do riot. You see it even in such circumstances as unemployment. The rival politicians rise to count heads as if the blame for unemployment among some Protestants was that there is not more unemployment among Catholics, thus hiding the essential issue that there is a scarcity of jobs, which is a matter for the whole people.

The mischief does not end there. This intimidation of mind enters every sphere of cultural life. The artist is shut in too. Writers who make their living in state or municipal employment have to be forever on guard over what they write, for Belfast has no body of professional writers who alone are free to reveal what they see in any country; and that freedom everywhere has its limitations too.

There is a cultural problem in Ireland deriving from a sectarian problem, and Irish writers are not as conscious as they should be. Is it they do not see, or that they dodge it?

A Diary of Events

When I left the Hibernian School, in the Phoenix Park, to return to Belfast, during the later period of the Boer War, I was young enough to be broad-minded in regard to religion and completely uninterested in political thought. I was fairly intelligent for my age and still retained the childish ideals of a fourteen years grown-up. But I was soon to lose those ideals.

I had lost my mother when I was five, and my father was now an invalid—and blind. I was the youngest of a family of six, three of whom had married. My father, an army pensioner, had found it somewhat difficult to support my brother and me on his meagre pension, but had managed to have me educated in the Hibernian School. I had only been home a year when my father died.

They say it is a dangerous habit to keep a diary of events and incidents in one's own life. This may be true in one sense, for some day it may reveal your shortcomings to other people's eyes. Few would care to face such a revelation, myself least of all.

But for many years I have kept a diary of events and incidents which taken place around me. Today, I find the diary both interesting and useful.

Forty years ago a Belfast shipyard labourer was lucky to carry home sixteen shillings as a week's wage. But tobacco was only threepence an ounce then, a pint of porter twopence, and a 'bap', which would have given a navvy a square meal, a penny. Kitchen houses were easily obtainable at half-a-crown. Parlour houses were four and sixpence. Working-class houses with baths were few and far between, and my family were lucky in moving into one of the first hundred. There were no accordion bands in the city. I don't even remember the existence of a pipe band. There were a number of brass and reed bands, and dozens of fife-and-drum combinations who played more by luck than tuition.

I became a member of a flute band which went by the title of 'Britannic Star Flute Band'. After several months practice, we managed four party tunes. We usually spent our Easter Mondays in a trip to Larne, returning to our rooms via Wellington Place and Great Victoria Street to Sandy Row. Incidentally, we timed our homeward journey to coincide with the return of a nationalist band from a GNR trip. On two occasions, we emerged out of the collision with all our drums burst.

Life for the young working-class people was somewhat empty of entertainment. There were no cinemas, few organised playing fields, and, with the exception of religious societies, no attempt to induce the youth of the country to fit themselves into healthy and useful citizens. So we grouped ourselves into 'clans'. There was the notorious 'Bogey Clan' with their camping ground in north Belfast. There was a row on the Crumlin Road one night and a youth died from his hurts. The police made a swoop on a certain day and the 'Bogey Clan' ceased to exist.

The 'Cronje Clan', who gathered somewhere in the neighbourhood of the Falls Road, were recognisable by their black-and-white checked caps, and named after a famous Boer general. The 'Forty Thieves', with headquarters in Church Street, were bitter enemies of the 'Cronje Clan'. They were not by any means vicious boys, but wild—oh! One of my brothers was a supporter of the 'Forty Thieves', and it was he who initiated me into the mysteries of gang warfare. I was soon able to whistle and sing 'The Boyne Water' and 'Dolly's Brae' without competition.

A riot would start after the conclusion of a football match played on the Bog Meadows, a great expanse of meadow land and brickfields situated between the Falls and Sandy Row, which would continue throughout the weekend, with recognised intervals for meals and sleep. The police generally let us knock hell out of each other so long as we kept away from inhabited districts. There was really no other form of entertainment for flaming youth at the time.

My first collision with the police occurred during the relief of Ladysmith celebrations. When the news of the relief arrived in Belfast the entire population downed tools and crowded the main thoroughfares to demonstrate. I was following a brass band in the procession along Royal Avenue when a shower of stones dropped amongst the crowd, thrown from the direction of Kent Street, a nationalist quarter. There was an immediate rush by the crowd towards this street, but the police were waiting for this eventuality. And so I had to record my first actual baton charge. There was a panic.

From my earliest days I was theatre-minded. I spent many enjoyable evenings in the old Theatre Royal and the new Opera House. Olga Nethersole brought Tolstoy's *Resurrection* to the Opera House. I had my great ambition fulfilled when I witnessed a performance by Sir Henry Irving in the dramatic version of *Faust*. I never missed a performance of Martin Harvey, Fred Terry or F.R. Benson when they visited Belfast. But one night in the old Theatre Royal I shall never forget. Forbes Robinson was giving his interpretation of Hamlet. As was usual on a Monday evening, the gallery was packed with newsboys, shipyard and factory hands. No women were allowed in the 'Gods' in those days.

Forbes Robinson held his audience spellbound for three solid hours. When he was brought to the footlights after the play, the gallery patrons rose instinctively to their feet and cheered frantically for some minutes. And the majority of the galleryites were illiterates or had spent few years at school.

I think it was those early days in Belfast theatre land which, some years later, stirred in me the desire to write industrial drama. I begged, borrowed, or stole the coppers which brought me my heart's desire—to see, and hear, and applaud the greatest exponents of dramatic art.

Of course, there was another side to the picture. Now and again, an Irish company would bring a repertoire of the real old rebel plays up north to the Theatre Royal. We weren't too sweet on this type of dramatic art, and generally collected a party of enthusiasts to patronise the performance, not so much to welcome the artists, rather to bring the play to an early conclusion. I was catch-boy in the shipyard at the time, and we filled our pockets with suitable missiles, such as bolts, rivets, half-bricks and such things.

There was one particular performance of *Arrah-na-Pogue* which I have cause to remember. We arrived in force at the theatre and occupied the centre of the gallery. We allowed the play to proceed until one of the actors broke forth into song. He managed to get through two lines of 'The Wearing of the Green' before we harmonised our voices into a rendering of 'The Boyne Water'. But we made a blunder that evening. The other side must certainly have had a warning of our visit. The battle only lasted five minutes, with the majority of my mates stretched out for the count. I was pretty small at the time and crawled between the legs of the contestants in an effort to get to the exit. A terrific kick in the pants sent me hurtling down the stone steps, seven at a time. Outside, we counted the survivors.

Thirty years after this incident, when *Castlereagh* was being produced by the Belfast Repertory Theatre, the director went round to Allen's in search of a suitable poster to illustrate the play on the hoardings. The choice was a rather dramatic incident in the original production of *Arrah-na-Pogue*.

There was no motor transport in Belfast at this period; horses supplied the haulage, both private and business. A good many of the smaller firms and warehouses kept small replicas of the standard two-wheeled cart in the form of a handcart. A youth was employed hauling the merchandise about in these. In case the public might be mistaken in the status of these youths, their employers gave them the title of 'porter', similar to that of the African coolie. I received six shillings a week during my own short contract.

It is curious that one should remember these minor incidents in the life of a single community whilst during the same period the rest of the world was steeped in war and revolution.

I have never been bored with city life. There is something glamorous, fantastic, unreal, about a great city teeming with life and vibrating with energy, which darkness barely compels to mark time till the dawn of another day. I never pass Royal Avenue without feeling that here you cleave through the soul of a great community.

One often hears the saying, 'Sure, there's nothing to see in Belfast! It's a dull place to live in!' I have never found it so, and off and on I have lived here during fifty odd years.

As a Child

Childhood and adolescence, if one could realise, have a bearing on one's character which exceeds any other influence in the making of a man's or woman's future life. If you grow up from childhood with a grudge against your fellow, it takes many, many years to soften the effects, and a lifetime to recapture all the happiness lost. Too many of us, reared in the cramped confines of an industrial city, commence life at a great disadvantage compared with that of our country friends.

We miss the beauty of the countryside, the fragrance of the flowers, the wild, heathery slopes of the hills, the music of the mountain streams. Even the hedges and haystacks have a meaning to every country-bred child, which you and I may never learn. Yet, I have often wondered if city life can compensate one for the loss of these precious things.

If I were to go back fifty years, when, as a child, I began to discover Belfast, there still remains a yearning in my heart for the excitement and adventure of those days. Little remains of the historic buildings which were scattered in and around the city centre. Even the lay-out of many familiar streets have changed.

For instance, the *Ulster Echo* and *Witness* office in Royal Avenue has disappeared. So have the small lock-up shops on the opposite side, where one could purchase an ounce of Irish-grown tobacco. 'The Century Bar', where Sinclairs now stands, and 'The Palace Bar', at the corner of North Street, were by no means ornaments to the city's architecture, compared to the present structures. Still, they were landmarks.

The south side of Castle Place retained a number of original town buildings—two-storied residential houses. Carter's Waxworks occupied one of these. One room at the back of the building was set aside as 'The Chamber of Horrors'. If my memory holds good, there was a tableau representing the murder of Terry, the actor, outside the stage door of a London theatre. Another was the gruesome spectacle of a murderer pushing his victim into the mouth of a furnace.

A circus of 'Flea Performers' held us spellbound, indulging in spectacular jumps and hauling tiny carts about. 'The Bearded Lady' and 'The Head without a body', were periodical visitors. I believe the admittance fee for children was twopence or threepence.

In my boyhood days, Donegall Road was always referred to as 'The Blackstaff.' Durham Street was 'Pound Loney.' 'Bower's Hill', now the Shankill Road. Ballynafeigh was known to us as 'The Brickfields'. The streets between Agincourt Avenue and Rugby Avenue was 'Holyland'; and stretching from there to Botanic Avenue was a wide expanse of grassland called 'The Plains', where many rising stars of future soccer fame made their debut.

'The Chapel Fields', stretching from Linenhall Street to Joy Street, was also a venue for football fans and, during the festive seasons, was crammed with roundabouts, circuses, wild beast shows and boxing booths. I remember some wild scenes here when the crowds got out of hand and the showmen had to defend their property with whatever weapons they could fashion.

Sunday afternoons in Summer, the old Bangor boat plied happily from Queen's Bridge jetty to Bangor and back. But the fare was beyond the pockets of us youngsters. So we 'bunched up' and chartered a rowing boat at the Sand Quay and sculled away to the Twin Islands for something like threepence a head.

Further up the Lagan, opposite the Ormeau Park, Tom Boyce ran a ferry across the river as well as letting out row-boats. We often rented a boat from Boyce's and rowed as far as Stranmillis weirs. There were few houses within sight of the river in those days, and the trip was a pleasant change from the streets.

After I left school and graduated into 'longs', I travelled further afield in my search for Greater Belfast. Ben Madigan, a name which is rarely applied to the Cavehill these days, was an adventurous trip. The Cavehill Road was a narrow thoroughfare, flanked on the left side by bogey lines which served the mountain limestone quarries, long out of use even then.

There had been a love tragedy at the foot of the quarry whilst I was still at school, when two youthful sweethearts sought spiritual union in death which was forbidden them in life. For many years some kindly passers-by would commemorate the sad event by drawing in limestone the initials of the two victims at the place of the tragedy. We youngsters always referred to the spot as 'Norah's Grave.'

On the summit of McArt's Fort, we discovered a seat hewn out of the solid rock, and overlooking Belfast Lough and the lovely Holywood hills. As children, it was known to us only as 'The Wearyman's Rest.' Many years later, when in conversation with the grand old Irish historian, the late F.J. Bigger, I mentioned this find, and was shocked at my own ignorance in not recognising it as the crowning chair of the chiefs of one of the Antrim branches of the O'Neills. The seat was practically demolished when I last stood on McArt's Fort.

One of our greatest discoveries was the 'Big Stone' at the top of the Glencairn Road. We filled our haversacks with buns and lemonade bottles and hiked it up the Ballygomartin. At the end of the Glencairn, we crossed the fields to the foot of the Gilbert Mountain where, in the centre of one of the fields, we reached our objective. It was many years later I discovered I had chalked my initials on the face of an ancient standing stone, which had been hoary with age long before the Gaels brought culture to pagan Ireland.

Belfast Fifty Years Ago

Half a century may not seem a wide gap in the life of a city, yet, in effect, it ages a city to the same extent as it does the individual citizen. Buildings, streets, habits, customs and entertainment all go through a phase of changeability that causes one who lived through fifty years of the scene, to wonder what fifty years hence will be like in regard to the city today. Admitting the fact that childhood and adolescent memories are apt to exaggerate the importance of communal life as it was and compare it to the present day standards, one wonders if progress is not after all a little too fast for the stability of most citizens.

Be that as it may, the city has overlapped its boundary posts to such an extent that its former green belt, which was fairly extensive in 1900-1, has now completely disappeared. Stranmillis, Upper Malone, Beechmount, Ballygomartin, Ardoyne, Ballysillan, Skegoniel, Whiterock, Cregagh and Knockbreda were outlying districts in my youthful days and only frequented as lovers' lanes. The Cavehill was accessible by way of the quarries or the Sheep's Path. The Shaftesbury estate wall ran the entire length of the Antrim Road from the Old Cavehill to the Sheep's Path. There was no Hazelwood or Bellevue in those days.

There were no electric trams, buses or taxi cabs. The old Irish jaunting car and hackney cab were always available at their stands around the city. The horse tram system, inaugurated less than thirty years previous to 1900, was a cumbersome and nerve-wracking mode of travelling. The tramcars were hauled around the city by a pair of powerful horses, supplemented by a tracer, ridden by a boy where a difficult hill had to be negotiated.

Clifton Street, the Crumlin and Ardoyne were traversed by relays of these tracers. Otherwise the tramcars would certainly have reversed their progress. The top platforms were inevitably open to the elements and, believe me, on a wild, winter's day this was a hair-raising experience.

Telephones may have been in use at the time, but there were certainly no telephone booths in the city. As a youth, I worked in several big warerooms and flax agents offices, yet I can't remember a telephone connection in any of these establishments. Speaking tubes were installed in many manor houses as well as factories. You blew down a pipe which caused a whistling sound at the other end. When your call was answered, you alternately spoke and listened through the same mouthpiece.

The top layer of the main thoroughfares was 'square-set', the side streets and footways were cobbled, more familiarly known as 'kidney pavers', and were used to some advantage against the RIC during the squabbles of the period. There were no tyred wheels in those days and the rumble of night traffic was sufficient to cause nightmares to the ordinary citizen.

In any case, work commenced at 6 am for most manual workers, and the streets resounded with tramping feet from 5 am onwards.

Kitchen houses were easily obtainable at half-a-crown a week; parlour houses were four and sixpence. Kitchenettes were unknown fifty years ago, and Devon grates had yet to be invented. Household bins were unknown, and the refuse of the 'middens' was, in the case of streets where there were no entries, often moved through the living-room to the street. Middens lay for weeks before being attended to, and how the health authorities stalled off disease is still a mystery to me.

Working-class food in those days was plain and, of necessity, cheap. Porridge, broth, stew, potatoes and buttermilk, without variation, was the daily subsistence. Cooking was done on the open grate, and the immense iron pots and kettles used then have disappeared. Home-baked soda scones and potato bread on the family griddle was the custom in every household. Coal wouldn't be more than a shilling a bag, perhaps cheaper. There were few gas ovens.

The younger generation fifty years ago read *Buffalo Bill, Dick Turpin, Comic Cuts, Pluck,* and the *Marvel.* Our elders were reading *The Redeemer* by Hall Caine; *Sherlock Holmes* by Conon Doyle; *She* by Rider Haggard. Evenings at home, we entertained by Edison Bell records on phonograph. The gramophone had not yet superseded this form of amusement. The phonograph records were, I admit, a bit scratchy, owing to the continuous playing.

Men wore bowler hats and caps in winter, straw hats and soft Panama hats in summer. Bare heads were not fashionable for men or women. Beards and mutton-chop whiskers were still retained by elderly people, but the rising generation were gradually breaking away from tradition and adopting the moustache alone as a facial ornament. Well-starched collars, three inches in breadth, kept the chin in position and made it almost a sacrifice to swallow.

There was no unemployment, health, or old-age pension insurance, and aged parents had a poor chance of finishing their life in comfort if their children were unable to support them. The veterans of the Crimean and Indian mutiny campaigns were still hobbling around, a number of the poor souls in the workhouse. After the conclusion of the Boer War, an effort was made to increase their pensions from ninepence to a shilling a day.

Public houses were open on Sundays as well as weekdays, and the spirit-grocer was an institution at the time. One half of the shop was a public-house, the other a grocer's shop, with no consumption on the premises. There were four Corporation public baths in the city in 1900—and they are still with us.

We had two theatres—the Opera House and the old Theatre Royal, and two music halls—the Alhambra and the Empire Theatre. Ginnett's Circus, in Glengall Street, had disappeared. The Theatre Royal was the home of Shakespearean drama, with F.R. Benson and Forbes Robinson as frequent visitors. Olga Nethersole, Fred Perry and Martin Harvey made the Opera House their Mecca.

The Exhibition Hall, Botanic Gardens, now part of Queen's University, was the rallying point for many political meetings. The Ulster Hall, still owned by a private company, was then, as now, the centre for orchestral and vocal concerts.

Castlereagh and James Hope, the weaver

Some years ago, I wrote a stage play dealing with the '98 period, in which the central characters were James Hope and Lord Castlereagh. The two men were so widely apart in social status, education, and ordinary everyday environment that I found it difficult to bring them together, even on the stage. The one was an aristocrat moving in the highest circles, the other an ordinary weaver by trade, living and toiling in the midst of his fellow workers.

James Hope held the confidence of the leaders of the United Irish movement, but he was never a member of the inner councils. Neilson, McCracken, Simms and Russell were middle-class citizens imbued with the ideal of freeing their country. Hope's ambition was to see his fellow workers living a decent and unfettered existence in their own land. Little is known of Hope's life until he threw in his lot with the United movement, yet he was respected and looked upon as a champion of the people's cause long before the United movement became popular.

Between the leaders of the organisation and the mass of the people was an almost insurmountable barrier of ignorance and dire poverty. Their only form of education was self-education, and even this form of ambition was looked upon with suspicion by the ruling classes. Still, there was the inevitable urge which most men possess in the search of knowledge. In Down and Antrim amongst the workers, especially the weaving fraternity, men were teaching themselves to read and write. It was to these men the poor landslaves and weavers turned for advice and instruction when trouble overwhelmed their families. It was to these the leaders of the United Irish Society appealed in their efforts to rouse the people.

Hope was a poet, so was James Orr of Ballycarry, who fought by Hope's side at the battle of Antrim. James Campbell of Larne was another. All weavers. None of these men were leaders, but they inspired those about them with their courage and loyalty. When the appointed day arrived to carry the ideals of the movement into battle, and Henry Joy McCracken, alone of the leaders, remained at his post, it was these stalwarts who clustered round his broken and disillusioned figure till the last.

When the fortunes of war turned almost certain victory into a disastrous rout, and the insurgent army battled for dear life in the streets of Antrim town, it was Hope and his companions who fought strenuously to save their leader from immediate capture and death. Even in the misery and defeat of a lost cause, leaders can obliterate their mistakes and leave a clean and courageous memory behind them. McCracken, helpless and with little hope of escaping certain death, insisted on the remnants of his army dispersing and seeking safety in flight.

When Castlereagh struck, his hand was heavy, but his scruples light. None understood better than he that without leadership the mass of the people were a helpless rabble. McCracken, Monro, and the Rev. James Porter of Greyabbey, were of a class he feared—the middle-class. They had friends and influence among the merchants of Belfast. Castlereagh realised these men were dangerous, and must at all costs be destroyed if his political scheming was to succeed.

Monro and McCracken were easy victims, but the Rev. James Porter was neither a participant in the rising nor a member of the United Society. Castlereagh never forgave a personal insult, and Porter had more than once held the Londonderry family up to public ridicule. A warrant on fabricated charges was soon procured against the reverend gentleman, and he was executed some weeks after the Battle of Antrim.

Castlereagh made one mistake. His contempt for the mass of the people allowed Hope, Orr and Campbell to escape his yeomen. These self-educated workers possessed more influence with the common people than even the most popular leader of the movement. They were the pioneers of something greater to come than ill-timed and unorganised revolt. In less than a century and a half, the descendants of these illiterate, landless, half-starved workers of the land and loom were to gain the power to make and unmake governments, whilst the aristocracy whom Castlereagh's sole aim was to perpetuate, was to pass into oblivion.

It may have been difficult for the Castle authorities to induce their paid informers to bear witness against Hope and the others. It may have been that Castlereagh had no wish to antagonise the mass of the people into personal hatred of himself.

James Hope was thirty-four years old when he carried his pike through Antrim town, with the responsibility of a wife and family. He was a strong adherent of the Presbyterian faith, and never wavered in that allegiance. Many of the clergy of his faith were implicated in the rising. Some perished, others were imprisoned, yet at no period did the revolt develop into a religious struggle.

Incidentally, I myself belong to the same denomination, and have had the privilege of worshipping in several of the meeting places where these men worshipped in their day. The present congregations, though they may disagree with the principles these men upheld, neither deny nor dishonour their memory.

Castlereagh, on the other hand, was baptised a Presbyterian in Dublin but his family soon realised that, if their son was to attain a prominent part in the affairs of the state, his denominational faith would be in the way. So the Presbyterian church saw him no more. No one can deny Castlereagh was a great statesman. He practically saved England from annihilation. When he died, surrounded as he was with wealth and power, few regretted his passing.

James Hope finished his long and industrious life in Brown Square, Peter's Hill. He died, as he lived, a weaver. At eighty-three, his intellect was still keen, his sturdy frame intact, his loyalty to his faith and the rights of his fellow-men as strong as ever. No participant in the turmoil of Irish history has left behind such a memory as this Templepatrick weaver. Monuments have been erected to greater figures in Irish history, but none to a greater man.

Flashbacks

Walking along Sandy Row a few days ago, I was struck by the great changes which have taken place in that thoroughfare since I was a child. The Brewery Building, with its magnificent ornamental gateway, still retains its massive Victorian architecture. Even as a child with an inquiring mind, I could never discover any Sandy Row inhabitant who could remember anything being brewed in the building. Yet I did miss the row of one-storied white-washed cottages which stretched from the corner of Hope Street right up to No. 22, where my grandfather lived for many years.

Then my memory flashed back fifty years to picture the Belfast of my childhood. Few Belfast citizens of the '90s of last century realised that, in their midst, were a number of young men who were soon to rise to great heights in their different professions. Robert Lynd, George Birmingham, James Douglas, John Lavery and St. John Ervine mixed with their fellow citizens in the neighbourhoods of Brookvale Avenue, Donegall Street, North Queen Street and the Short Strand without attracting undue notice.

The town had just been raised, by Charter, to rank as a city, and a new spirit of progress and adventure was stirring many of its young ambitious citizens.

I saw the last of the Cromac Water carts, with its horse drawn container, selling water in the streets at so much a bucket. Occasionally a herd of nanny goats would be driven through the streets, whilst their owners ladled out pure fresh milk at a penny a pint.

My family lived for a time in the Donegall Pass district where most of the gasworkers resided. Gas was so expensive at the time we all used paraffin for illumination. Some of the lamps were of beautiful design in metal and glass, but many old people suffered premature blindness through eye strain. The Jewish population of the city lived in this neighbourhood well into the early days of the present century, as their synagogue had not yet been occupied by the Independent Orangemen.

Cromac Street at that period was a mixed locality. Little May Street, Hamilton Street and Henrietta Street were inhabited, in the main, by Protestant families. A number of my father's relatives lived there. I attended a Protestant infant school at the corner of Eliza Street, which, if my memory serves me, was named 'Haslett's School'. Afterwards, most of these families removed to 'The Plains', when the district became a built-up area.

Tom Boyce, whose family had been in the service of Lord Donegall when that nobleman resided at his Ormeau demesne, retained the sole rights to ferry the public from River Terrace across the Lagan to the pier on the Ormeau bank.

From his boathouse he also rented out rowboats to the public who could ply up-river as far as Stranmillis locks. We youngsters would bunch up a shilling between us and rent one of his boats for a Sunday afternoon's trip as far as the weirs, where we generally had a swim in the broadwater beneath. Tom Boyce was one of the foremost boxers of his days and none of us tried funny tricks with his boats.

'The Plains', comprising many acres of flat, grassy land between Botanic Avenue and Rugby Avenue, was the rendezvous of junior football enthusiasts. On a Saturday afternoon, thousands of spectators would gather to cheer their different clubs from Sandy Row or 'The Pass.' During the 1890s 'The Plains' was one of the largest open spaces in Belfast. Today there isn't any space left for building, let alone sport.

When I was a child there were only three legitimate theatres in the city; the old Theatre Royal, the Alhambra, and the Empire Theatre. Ginnett's Circus occupied the space where the Opera House now stands, and its Saturday matinee was a boon to us youngsters, for the price of admission never ranged higher than a penny or twopence. When I left school and received permission to attend performances in the Theatre Royal, threepence admitted me to the gallery, and even the Grand Circle was reasonable at a shilling.

'McCormick's Show', which operated between the Shankill and Old Lodge roads as a theatre of sorts, staged plays from Shakespeare to *Murder at the Red Barn*. I was too young during its existence to travel far from my own district and, by the time I had grown independent of my parents, the 'show' had closed down.

At the beginning of the present century half an hour's quick walking could land you practically at the outskirts of the city. Stockman's Lane and 'The Finaghy Loney' were pleasant country walks with only a few cottages ornamenting the landscape. The Stranmillis finished its city appearance a little beyond Friar's Bush Cemetery, and a glassworks was established in the hollow as you turned into the Lockview Road to reach the river. After passing Tate's Avenue, on the Lisburn Road, one was almost in the open country, stretching away to the foot of the Divis Mountains.

The South African war was at its height when I left school, and I was working in a local factory when news came through that Mafeking had been relieved. When the news reached Belfast there were scenes of unparalleled enthusiasm. Hysterical crowds surged through the centre of the city, rockets soared into the sky and bands formed an unending procession. Armistice Day in 1918, and the 1945 VE celebrations were mere demonstrations compared to 'Mafeking Day'. Yet there were perhaps no more than a hundred casualties during the entire Mafeking siege.

During the early 1900s, an exciting competition was initiated by the *Ulster Saturday Night* to discover which of the local senior football teams had the most numerous following. The newspaper office was almost swamped with voting papers. When the votes were finally counted, Ra Torrens, the Linfield captain, was first, Sam Burnison, the Distillery captain, second, and J. Pyper, the Cliftonville captain, third. Each of the captains was presented with a valuable prize by the proprietors. By the way, 'The Pink' in those days was really pink in colour.

It is curious how minor passing events like these remain in one's memory when other episodes of national and political importance are forgotten and left to historians to record.

Melodrama Days

The exciting days of melodrama in the theatre is now past history. Most of us—I mean the older generation—have practically forgotten it ever existed. The younger generation of theatre goers have missed the treat of their lives. Still, with the amateur dramatic societies getting into harness for the coming season, one may be forgiven for drawing their attention to the easy passage they have in producing a play compared with the obstacles which confronted their predecessors fifty or sixty years ago.

The old Theatre Royal, in Arthur Street, was the only venue of these spectacular and interesting plays. When the Royal Cinema replaced that theatre, melodrama died a natural death. Looking back on those early days, one has to admit the fact that the fast-moving plots and ingenious settings far outstripped the most elaborate productions of these modern times. A collision at sea, with appropriate mountainous waves, lashing spray, and wind at hurricane force, was child's play to the stage hands.

I remember one production where the climax of an act was a steam-hammer thumping down on a moving platform to which the heroine was bound hand and foot. Luckily, at each performance, the hero dashed in breathless, released his beloved and hauled her clear, just as the hammer was on the point of crushing her adorable head. What would have happened had he been a second or two late I haven't the faintest conception. I only know, the audience gave a gasp of relief and broke out into hoarse cheers.

Another play which I recollect was entitled *Is Life Worth Living?* In this production, a real steam-roller went around the stage. The producer of this true-to-life drama was doubtful regarding the credulity of his audience to realise that the steam-roller was a factual element in the scene, had the following notice printed on the programme: "The steam-roller used in Act II has been specially constructed for Mr. Hulbert by the celebrated engineers, Messrs. Aveling & Port, at their works in Rochester."

Mechanical representation was by no means the only device used to attract an audience. Animals, both wild and tame, were occasionally paraded on the boards. When *The Still Alarm*, an American fire-fighting play, was produced at the old Theatre Royal in the '90s of last century, a pair of well-bred Arab horses pranced around the stage, complete with fire engine. One of our local theatrical critics had this to say: "A fire engine station at New York seems to be an ideal place for a midnight lounge. It happens (according to the author) when the firemen return to their quarters after a hard day's work at a terrible conflagration, they have a musical rehearsal and sing sentimental songs, combined with the attraction of a circus, a street preacher and a glee club."

In *A Royal Divorce*, which continued to draw an audience in Belfast until World War II, Napoleon was always present during a spectacular scene depicting the Battle of Waterloo, seated astride a white charger, with the Old Guard around him. The curtain dropped for a few seconds, then was raised to show him leading his army in full retreat with the English forces in full pursuit. In this scene he was dismounted, his charger being held by a soldier. Actually Napoleon escaped from the battlefield in a carriage.

As for 'thriller!' The most gruesome thriller I ever witnessed, *The Face at the Window*, a detective play with a French setting, was a regular visitor to the Arthur Street theatre. The detective was fatally stabbed, but before he died he managed to scribble down, using his own blood as ink, the first few letters of his attacker's name. In a later scene, his dead body was laid on a platform, and a doctor arrived carrying an electric contraption, which he proceeded to attach to the dead body. There was a whirr of machinery, then the dead man's hand gradually came to life, and with the original strip of paper conveniently placed, the dead man's hand completed the name of his assailant. Talk about suspense!

Dion Boucicault's great Irish plays were always sure of a popular welcome in Belfast. In most of these Irish productions, a huge cast was necessary, with elaborate settings. In *The Shaughraun*, there were no less than seventeen characters, and although it was a mere three-act play there were sixteen changes of scenery. This was an easy production compared with *The Silver King*, which retained a cast of twenty-three, not to mention the crowd of 'supers', such as clerks, railway officials, passengers, detectives and children. I witnessed *The Silver King* on two occasions and still wonder how they managed to enforce stage directions with such a crowd.

Few plays will now be accepted by theatre directors if they call for more than one or two changes of scenery, and to suggest anything like an open sea act, a steam-roller, or even a pair of mules on stage would only cause amusement or ridicule. In fact, a playwright would be well advised to repeat the same scene right through his play. Yet in revue, pantomime, opera or variety shows, it is the common practice to vary the scenery which, I think, could be well followed in drama. After all, the activities of men and women are not centred in any one particular spot. In melodrama the action of the play was spread occasionally half-way round the world.

Bite, Bark and Swallow

Forty years ago I was a young man, full-blooded, adventurous, straining at the leash, ready to bark, bite and swallow anything that might come my way. I was interested in sports, theatres and reading. Young ladies were not too expensive to take around and I enjoyed their company. Cafés were non-existent at the time, cinemas had barely passed their 'living picture' days. Yet life was by no means dull. Politics were a much more amusing topic of interest to young men than they are today. To give our present young bloods an idea of how we old fellows spent our wasted lives forty years ago, here are a few extracts from an old diary of mine dated 1905:

Sunday—th March—Spent the afternoon walking round the Custom House steps. Immense crowds assembled to listen to half a dozen orators, quack doctors and lay preachers. Vendors of 'welks', 'bulls eyes', and 'yellow man' doing a great trade. Afterwards, Jim and I, stroll along the quayside watching the sailors aboard the cross channel steamers and admiring the sailing ships at York Dock. We travel as far as 'The Twin Islands' then turn back home.

Monday—Went to political meeting at Shaftesbury Square 7.30. About 2,000 people gathered.

Tuesday—It's painful rising out of bed at 5 am in the morning to reach the shipyard for 6 am. I wonder will our dreams of a 8 am start ever come true. 8 pm, I meet Maud at Shaw's Clock, at the corner of Sandy Row and Lisburn Road. Bought a penny packet of pop corns. Maud was all delighted. Kept us chewing the whole evening. We had a lovely walk along Stranmillis. Very few houses after, we pass Friar's Bush Cemetery. Ditches on both sides of the road after you pass Stranmillis House.

Wednesday—Went to Theatre Royal in Arthur Square. Paid threepence and managed a fine seat in the gallery. Saw a few of the town's big-wigs in the grand circle. The seats are very expensive in the circle—one shilling each. I suppose the big-wigs have pots of money to spend. The upper circle cost sixpence and the pit fourpence. The play this week is *The Face At The Window*. We were held spellbound with three murders, and the detective brought back to life through some electric contraption, long enough to write down the name of the murderer before he returns to his Heavenly abode. I should enjoy a grisly nightmare tonight.

Thursday—Went to the 'Cornhill, Tailors', Upper North Street, to pick up my new suit. They're easily the best tailors in Belfast. It was a perfect fit. I don't begrudge the cost—nineteen shillings and sixpence, although it's a lot of money for a tailored suit. I meet Maud at Pim's Clock corner of Donegall Pass and Dublin Road. We walk along Botanic Avenue only to spot her father and mother on opposite side. We had to fly for our lives. Thank goodness they didn't notice Maud.

She would have received a fair hiding. Maud is just past seventeen, and her parents are very respectable.

Friday—We are very busy down at the shipyards just at present. Immediately after a ship is launched they are preparing to lay a new keel. I met the rest of the boys for football practice on 'The Plains', at Rugby Avenue. There were four or five other teams scattered about the fields. The treasurer collected our membership dues—one penny per week per member. We have a satisfactory balance in hand, nine shillings and sixpence. That sum may be sufficient to pay for our football rigs next week.

Saturday—The boys are in great form. We played Shankill Rovers on the football pitch at Peter's Hill, in front of Brown Square Police Barracks, and won 4-2. There was a big crowd of spectators, but the police had an easy time keeping order. They did draw their batons three times to clear the pitch when we looked like winning, but with the exception of the referee having to be carried off the field. I don't think there were many serious casualties.

The good old days! What.

Odyssey of an 'Out-of-Work' in the 1930s

When World War I broke out and many of my shipyard mates joined up there was soon a shortage of semi-skilled workers in the yards. I made an application and was granted a hand-driller's kit. Most outside boilershop work was allotted to repairing warships. It was interesting work, but the hours were too long and the labour rather tedious. Although with overtime and war bonus, we generally managed a wage packet of three or four pounds every week, a hand-driller's basic wages was still as low as twenty-five shillings a week.

It was my first experience earning big money yet, with the prices of essential commodities soaring skywards, this meant little difference to the worker's standard of living. In any case, the war fever had got into my blood and I threw in the driller's kit and joined the Royal Engineers. A sapper in the Engineers received two shillings and twopence a day in 1914. At least, that was the bait. The army authorities forgot to pay me anything for the first two months, and by that time I was sitting on the Menin Road with every ounce of patriotic zeal scared out of me.

I was demobbed during the latter part of 1919 without any particular mention of distinguished conduct to my army record, and I returned to the shipyard. Meanwhile machinery had progressed to such an extent that riveting and drilling was now automatic, and hand-drilling was an ancient craft. I had been promised my job would be retained for me after hostilities had ceased. It was.

The following month there was a pay-off in the yard and, for the first time in my life, I was on the 'dole'. Being an ex-serviceman, with a family, I was supposed to receive preferential treatment. My unemployment allowance was twenty-nine shillings a week. This lasted six months, then you applied for an extended benefit. A family man was generally lucky. Meanwhile the foreman gave me a tip that I had a poor chance regarding my driller's kit, so I offered myself as a 'helper'. Shipyard wages were at their peak about this time and a 'helper's' rate had mounted to three pounds nine shillings, including war bonus. During my idle months it never struck me to try any other source of employment. I preferred the shipyard to any other type of labour. Another pay-off in eleven months' time showed me the fallacy of being tied to one particular job.

I soon tired of standing by the shipyard gates every morning for countless days with a forlorn hope that my name might be called out as a 'start'. Then I commenced a routine visit at several big firms in the city offering my services. Generally you received a kindly reception, but even employers became exasperated at the repetition of "any chance this morning, Sir?" Meanwhile unemployment figures had risen to 50,000, and were continuing to rise in Northern Ireland. Craftsmen were now competing with labouring men for any type of manual work. With odd spells of from three weeks to nine months in the shipyards throughout a period of five years, my unemployment benefit looked like disappearing altogether.

The 'Glass House' where you were interrogated regarding your prospects of finding work, was in full swing. This was a type of 'Star Chamber', where local barristers put you through a cross-examination, something after the procedure of a criminal court. It depended on the 'court's' report whether you received any further benefit. The 'means test' was in full operation at the time. I attended a meeting of protest at the Gallery Cinema, sponsored by the unemployed, when T. Henderson MP and the late Alderman Byrne spoke against this method of depriving the workless of their benefits. It was of little avail.

Then followed the 1929-32 slump in world trade. If the previous years were lean, we were now up against the real thing. The Union Workhouse was already overcrowded. Outdoor relief, or, as it came to be popularly called ODR, became an institution. If you had run out of your unemployment benefit, you made application for outdoor relief. This meant you were put on relief work at eight shillings a day. You weren't allowed to earn more than twenty-eight shillings in any one week. Instead of being paid in cash, you received a 'chit' for the amount which you presented to your grocer who gave you the equivalent in goods. Out of pure kindness, an odd grocer, would return you a few shillings to pay your rent. Still, he was running a risk.

When the ODR men went on strike against their bitter position a wave of sympathy spread through the city on their behalf. Employers and traders were lavish in their gifts to assist them in their helpless struggle. Food and monetary assistance poured into their common fund, making it possible to press their grievances against the cruel standards they were forced to live under.

Meanwhile, Workman & Clark's shipyard had closed its gates for ever and my chances of getting back into industry were by no means rosy. I was offered an opportunity to start a one-man business on my own which about saved my life and reason at the time. I considered this a stroke of luck. I didn't realise what I was tackling. A wage-earner all my life, without any serious responsibility, I came to understand the trials of a one-man business. And I did not like it. Still, I was free from shattering doubts and uncertainties of the unemployment queues and my mind was occupied with problems which gave me little time for idleness.

The small office I rented was surrounded by other small offices. An artist, a poster writer, a photographer, all were having the same troubles to make ends meet on as meagre a capital as I was myself. I was receiving sympathy and encouragement from people as badly off as myself. I was learning to face life with a philosophy quite new to my outlook. I can't say I enjoyed the experience, but it was worthwhile. When I was forced to admit failure and return to manual labour, it was with a clearer reasoning power and a broader outlook on life.

I tried my hand at a dozen different occupations—gardening, painting, dealing, but succeeded only in one effort. I discovered I could express myself to some extent in prose and poetry, and the press were more than considerate. I was able to stand upon my own two feet until I found steady employment. Travelling along the hard road is not a pleasant journey, but you meet some grand fellows whom otherwise you may have missed. And it would be a pity to leave this life without having met them.

The Good Old Days in Belfast

City life has never been tiresome for me. Looking back sixty odd years, Belfast has given me some exciting moments. The city has spread, the population has increased, customs have changed, but life goes on as before. Tragedy, comedy and farce continuing to shape the life of the individual citizen. Commonplace events of today become historical facts in a hundred years' time. You or I may become spectators or participants in some particular incident which may effect the life of the whole community yet in a day or a week or a month the episode has passed from our minds and history has lost most valuable data.

My earliest recollections of the city of my birth, though somewhat obscured and hazy because of my tender years, are of the old White Linen Hall in the glory of a summer's day, with it's cool and shady grounds festooned with stately foliage, jealously watching the inevitable destruction of what was at one time the aristocratic residential quarter of the city. I lived in Little May Street then, and we children, had fun and frolics round the railed enclosure of the old building. The Chapel Fields, too, were our playground. The Fields were bordered by Ormeau Avenue and stretched from Joy Street to Linen Hall Street. For many years they were used as a fair ground at Christmas and Easter holidays.

I spent a few nights in what had been my grandparents home in Sandy Row, a small, single-storied white-washed cottage with its half door, which stood, one of a row of similar dwellings right on the corner of Hope Street. The Brewery Buildings, with its fine, ornamental entrance, often held me spellbound. Even in my childhood days I could never discover any Sandy Row man who remembered the brewery working.

The Bog Meadows stretched from Broadway across to the GNR embankment with Roden Street, then half built, its southern boundary. Ballynafeigh was a straggling suburb, with Ravenhill a wilderness beyond My Lady's Road. The Stranmillis, Stockman's Lane and Finaghy were lovers' lanes. Ligoniel was 'a brave wee dander' from Ardoyne Chapel through picturesque country scenery.

Tremendous crowds gathered at the Custom House steps to hear Arthur Frew and Tom Sloan orate on behalf of their militant organisations, whilst an occasional procession on the 15th August sent the heat wave through the city which brought hurried reinforcements of the RIC from their depots.

About 1906, Captain Shaw Taylor and Lord Dunraven came to the Ulster Hall to propound their Devolution scheme to settle the Home Rule question. The hall was packed with unionists, nationalists, independents, and the adherents of a political group which was gaining many converts, the Labour Party. The meeting developed into a party debate, the audience taking sides, cheering or groaning as individual speakers from the body of the hall jumped to their feet and let off steam.

Politics, forty or fifty years ago in Belfast, were much more important to the individual citizen than entertainment or sport. In fact, a political meeting in those days, held at a similar hour to a football match, would have ruined 'the gate' receipts.

Tom Sloan became MP for South Belfast in 1902, defeating a member of the landowning class. Sloan was an Island man, and the first working-man to represent a Belfast seat at Westminster. His supporters founded the Independent Orange Order. A Dublin Orangeman, R. Lindsay Crawford, threw in his lot with the Independents and was eventually elected Grand Master. Crawford was a Protestant, being editor of the *Irish Protestant*, a Dublin Journal. He was a fine orator, but ran foul of the official party when he took over the editorship of the local Liberal organ, the *Ulster Guardian*. He supported the Belfast dockers during the dock strike of 1907, and presided at one of Jim Larkin's meetings. Even the Independent couldn't abide this presumption and he was expelled. Later he emigrated to Canada, thence to the USA, where he joined the Irish movement. On the foundation of the Irish Free State, he became their trade representative in America.

During the 1906 General Election, when the Liberal Party was returned with a huge majority, Belfast was boiling over with political enthusiasm. Fierce battles raged in the south, north and west divisions. In the north, a Labour nominee, Willie Walker, was narrowly beaten by a few hundred votes. His opponent was Sir Daniel Dixon. Tom Sloan again defeated the Unionist, Lord Arthur Hill, by 810 votes and, in the west, Joseph Devlin, to everyone surprise, won the seat by the narrow margin of 16 votes against his Unionist opponent, Mr. Boyd-Carpenter. In the 1910 General Election, the official party trounced their opponents with the exception of Joseph Devlin, who retained his seat.

The days of the Home Rule controversy were packed with vivid and colourful scenes in Belfast, and many of the personalities taking part were prominent public figures in national life. On the occasion of Winston Churchill's visit to Celtic Park, when he was a Liberal Home Ruler, I happened to be on the working staff of the now defunct *Ulster Echo* in Royal

Avenue. My lunch hour coincided with the appearance of Churchill and his wife at the doors of the Grand Central Hotel. An angry mob swirled round his car and, but for a sudden rush of the police to his rescue, there would have been no Churchill on the platform of the Celtic Park meeting. I never in all my experience witnessed such a hostile reception as Churchill received that afternoon as he drove off to the meeting.

Occasionally the struggle for political supremacy was carried into the municipal arena, and a political feud would rage for weeks in one of the city wards. One of the fiercest battles I can recollect was staged in St. George's Ward, about 1904, the cockpit of which was Sandy Row. Sir James Henderson's opponent on this occasion was Tom Sloan, the sitting member for the parliamentary division. Bands and banners, waggons and brakes crowded Sandy Row night after night. Crowds yelled defiance at each other, and police held the warring forces apart. Half the city population ranged themselves on either side as if the fate of the entire country depended upon the result of the election. Tom Sloan was defeated by a majority of 98 votes. That evening, the police were on the alert in case war might be declared by one side or the other.

Nobody was really hurt. It was just another grand slam. With no cinemas, ballets, musical festivals, and only a few theatres to entertain the population, there was no other outlet for our ordinary human emotions, and so we took our politics seriously in those days.

The Story of Sandy Row

Sandy Row may be a somewhat common name for one of our most densely populated and thriving shopping centres, but the place it holds in the history of Belfast and the story of the city's expansion is far from commonplace. True, the name has no meaning when compared with other districts like the Shankill, Falls, Malone, Ligoniel or Ballynafeigh, nor can it claim the significance of thoroughfares like the Antrim, Crumlin, Newtownards or Lisburn roads. Yet it has an importance out of all proportion to its area.

The story of Sandy Row is the history of a small community which grew up on the outskirts of Belfast towards the middle of the eighteenth century.

It was cut off from the town by the then broad waters of the Blackstaff River, but being on the main road to Dublin, and nestling on the south bank of the river immediately after crossing the Salt Water Bridge (now the Boyne Bridge), it increased in importance because of the traffic which flowed across the bridge into the town from Lambeg, Lisburn, Dromore, Newry and as far south as Dublin.

At first, it was a mere row of one-storied cottages a few yards distant from the main road, with the tidal waters of the Lagan meeting the fresh water of the Blackstaff, and thus forming a little sandy cove where the labourers wives washed their linen, and the children paddled to their hearts' content.

The driver of the mail coach from Dublin, once he had passed the toll gates at Malone, speeded up his horses as he raced through Sandy Row, across the Salt Water Bridge into the Pound Loney, swerved right into Hamill Street and Castle Street, to pull up at the Donegall Arms in High Street.

When the new Lisburn Road was constructed early in the last century, the tollgates were moved back to the corner of Sandy Row and the new road, Sandy Row, by this time had extended almost to the toll house.

Half-way through the 1830s rumours swept into the quiet lives of the people that a great railroad was to be constructed as far as Lisburn, with an immense terminus to be erected beyond Sandy Row. The inhabitants couldn't believe their ears. To them it was the end of the world.

By the end of 1839, Sandy Row had this rail barrier added to the Blackstaff, separating the district from the town. More disastrous still was the construction of a new road running from Fisherwick Place to 'The Pass'— Great Victoria Street. Sandy Row had ceased to function as a main road.

Up till now the male population had been employed on railroad construction or shaping the new thoroughfare. With these finished, the inhabitants had a lean time until the advent of the Ulster Brewery and flax mills at Linfield Road and Tea Lane. Although Tea Lane had already lost its identity in Rowland Street, the mill was still referred to as 'Tay Lane' Mill when I was a child.

It was during the '50s and '60s of the last century that the inhabitants of the rural areas adjoining commenced their influx into the industrial centres. Streets of these small kitchen houses so familiar to Belfast were springing up like mushrooms in the Sandy Row area.

Families from the outlying districts would pile their belongings on to a country cart coming into the town—for rail transport was beyond the pockets of these country folk—and unload at the first working-class area they came to, hoping that all would be well with them. There was work in the mills, factories, and shipyards, and, to them, higher wages than the land could possibly offer.

Sandy Row was Eldorado to these folk from Lambeg, Lisburn, Hillsborough and Dromore. They would travel all night, and possibly land in Belfast on a bleak, frosty morning, before an empty house in one of the back streets of that district. All they could hope for was a kindly welcome.

It was in 1861 that my grandfather left his cottage in Drumbo, joined the stream and settled at No. 18 Sandy Row. In my early years in Sandy Row practically every family residing there had connections with the country.

Where previously the Blackstaff had separated the district from the town, the railway now added another barrier. The railway company constructed a branch forking from Utility Street to the foot of the Lisburn Road, thus isolating the community and enclosing the entire district in a 'band of steel', with only two outlets, a bridge over the river and railway at Durham Street, and a pedestrian bridge over the Railway at Utility Street. But Sandy Row continued to grow.

During the late 1870s, Sandy Row was destined to make history in the field of sport. At the top of Linfield Road was Linfield mill with an expanse of field attached. The hecklers and roughers of the mill who had been using the field in leisure hours approached the directors for permission to form a football team and the use of the ground as a playing field. The directors, not without misgivings, gave permission and this was the starting point of a club that has one of the finest records in Ulster sport—Linfield.

From its earliest days, Sandy Row has remained an exclusively working-class district, with a strong Protestant and Orange background. It has been the cockpit of many election battles. When the district was part of the South Belfast division, it was in the Sandy Row area that the parties fought it out. Now the same applies to the west division.

Bars and Circuses

In my boyhood days, just before the South African War, when the cinema industry had still to reach its infancy, and even commercial theatres were scarce, the Belfast public had a lean time in their search for entertainment.

My earliest recollection of Belfast entertainment, outside the ordinary theatres, was a local minstrel troupe which gave performances all over the province.
Earlier, as a child, my eldest brother was in the habit me of bringing me to Fred Ginnett's Circus, where the Opera House now stands. I can't for the life of me remember whether it was a canvas tent, or a corrugated or permanent building. I know the admission fee for the children's matinee was a penny and twopence. The Opera House was built in 1898, and Ginnett's Circus ceased to be.

In the early part of the present century McCormick's Show, situated first at Spier's Place, where the fire station was afterwards erected, then at McTier Street, between the Shankill and Old Lodge Roads, became the rendezvous of working-class patrons. In this small theatre one could see a repertoire of plays, ranging from *Murder in the Red Barn* to *Macbeth*. The admission price was a penny, twopence and threepence. The penny patrons were compelled to stand, the threepenny portion of the audience sat on the front forms. You paid 'the lady' at the door. Occasionally the house was uproarious.

The Alhambra, built in the early '70s of the last century, was originally a Victorian music hall, erected for Dan Lowry, an Irish comedian. Whilst I was still a youngster, the late W.J. Ashcroft had taken over control and brought it up to modern requirements. It had a prosperous, though sometimes riotous existence, until Ashcroft's death, when it finally developed into its present status as a cinema. I only witnessed W.J. in one performance, his farewell to his many Belfast admirers. I was quite young at the time, but it was a murderous adventure gaining admission that evening.

The present Empire Theatre, built in 1895, occupies the site of the old 'Buffalo Hotel and Music hall'. The Buffalo was a Victorian style music hall, where you paid for a frothy pint of porter, sat down in a vacant seat, and enjoyed a variety performance of sorts. I wasn't old enough to hit the Buffalo during its lifetime, but I did manage to visit the last Victorian music hall in the city, before the phase completely disappeared. The present building occupied by the R.A.O.B. in Church Street, was 'The Star Music Hall' about fifty years ago. The proprietor was a gentleman who afterwards became a Stormont MP. He was a prominent figure in the anti-prohibition crusade.

Licensed premises at the time were allowed to open after church hours on Sunday evening. Visiting 'The Star', you also paid for your drink, carried it through to the concert hall, laid your glass beside you on a pew-shaped form, and applauded. The chairman thumped the table for order, then invited volunteers from amongst the audience to oblige. The pianist thumped out a few bars and the performer set the pace for the discordant harmony which followed. The Star eventually developed into a boxing salon with the same price of admission, before it joined its predecessors in oblivion.

Before my time, there were a number of these free and easy public places of entertainment spread around the centre of the town. I can only give a hazy picture of how they appeared to the visitor. A raised platform stood at one end of the room with a much abused piano pushed to one side. You paid for your drink and joined the audience. The chairman called for "Order, gentlemen, please", introduced the pianist, then appealed to one of his nearest neighbours to oblige with a number. Let the vocalist be good, bad or indifferent, there was always an encore. The chairman insisted, applause or no applause. Usually the floor was covered with a carpet of sawdust a few inches thick. If not, spitoons were spread across the floor like so many flower pots, and were brought into use when the occasion demanded.

In Chichester Street was the 'Hippodrome', which, if I remember correctly, was housed in a temporary building. Here I witnessed a hair-raising feature, 'Looping the Loop', when a stunt motor-cyclist raced his motor-cycle round and round an upright hoop-track which placed him upside down during the most part of his daring performance. I remember, too, many local boxers facing each other in the Hippodrome, when the management gave a session over to their sporting fans. When the Royal Hippodrome opened in 1907, its Chichester namesake disappeared.

It would be a pity to pass over the Coliseum, at the corner of Grosvenor Road and Durham Street. In its early days, it was the Alexandra Theatre. I am not certain whether it opened first as a variety hall or drama centre. I do remember it was erected as a theatre and staged plays there occasionally. I witnessed variety shows there, too, before it came under the cinema hammer.

Belfast in '98

Belfast, on the eve of the rebellion of 1798, was in a tumult of anticipation. Its population of some 20,000 souls, though overawed and harassed by a strong force of military and badgered by the zeal of patriotic adherents of the Castle authorities, moved about the street giving sullen and unwilling obedience to the muskets and bayonets of the yeomen. Martial law would soon be driving them into their homes and holding them prisoners there till their compatriots outside the town were victorious or destroyed.

The town had been cordoned off from the surrounding countryside and few could get in or out except by permission or pass. The three bridges across the river into County Down: the Long Bridge, at Belfast; the Red Bridge, situated beyond Molly Ward's Locks on the far reaches of the Lagan; and Shaw's Bridge, which led to Saintfield and Ballynahinch, were easily blocked. The Carrickfergus, Shankill, Falls and Malone Roads were the only exits from the town into the country. The Antrim, Crumlin and Lisburn Roads had yet to be constructed.

Despite the ring of steel around the town, Jimmy Hope, the Templepatrick weaver, slipped through the cordon, collected a stack of pikes, and tricked his way out again. Local United men had fled the town earlier to escape the floggings that were being carried out daily, and joined the comrades at Carnmoney, where the insurgents were rallying in large numbers.

The authorities realised that if they could isolate Belfast where the republican spirit was rampant, they might succeed in striking at the heart of the conspiracy. It was here where the United movement had originated and the plan of campaign arranged. Those leaders who had escaped imprisonment were hiding somewhere in the town. The yeomen's purpose was to hold them there till the insurgent forces were crushed in the country.

The First, Second and Third Presbyterian meeting houses in Rosemary Street stood silent and deserted as the redcoats patrolled up and down the streets. But their congregations crouched behind the doors of their homes, alert and watchful. There was no need to inform them that with dawn of another day would come 'the rising'. The 'word' had already been whispered from mouth to mouth, from house to house.

Even the Scottish shipwrights, whom William Ritchie had brought over with him from Glasgow to found the new shipyard on the north bank of the

Lagan, were not unsympathetic to the ideals of their Irish brethren. Ritchie himself was a member of the second congregation.

With the dawn of the 7th June, came the tidings of the rising. The green flag of the insurgents had been raised at Carnmoney, and the march on Antrim had begun. Rumours spread and the population crowded out of the alleys, lanes and courts into the main streets, only to be driven back into their homes and ordered to remain indoors under the penalty of being shot. For the time being, at any rate, the Catholic was not considered as dangerous as the Covenanter.

As the day wore on, the town became subdued and quiet. With no news from the outside, doubts assailed the citizens that all was not well. The movement of large forces of cavalry and infantry out of the town meant reinforcements for the government troops. Then prisoners began to arrive, escorted by jubilant yeomen, and the townspeople realised the worst. The insurgents had been defeated.

The people cowered in fear as the soldiers battered in their doors with the butt-ends or rifles and demanded the names of absent members of the family. House to house searches went on, irrespective of the plight of any household who may have had feeble or sick persons in the family.

Many merchants and tradesmen who had been foremost in vaunting their republican ideals now slunk into the background. Others recanted under slight pressure. A few tried to reason with the now violent yeomen, determined on wreaking vengeance upon the citizens who had never submitted to their pompous and callous authority.

For the next few days, the hangings and floggings and burnings went on apace. No citizen's life was safe who had shown sympathy, either physical or verbal, to the cause of the insurgents. Word was somehow passed out to the Belfastmen who had taken part in the outbreak not to return to their homes at the peril of their lives. The scaffold, at the corner of the Cornmarket, was in great demand just at the moment.

On the shrub-covered slopes of the Belfast mountains, Henry Joy McCracken was pleading with Jimmy Hope and the remnants of the insurgent army to disperse to their home or flee the country.

Undaunted to the last, Jimmy Hope and his few remaining stalwarts refuse to desert their leader, until reason showed them the utter futility of attempting another stand against overwhelming odds.

With the defeat of the Down insurgents at Ballynahinch a few days later, the final wreck of the national movement in Ulster was complete. Belfast never regained its political importance as a stronghold of national vigour and idealism. Whilst the bitterness of the '98 revolt lingered, the townspeople still retained their tolerance towards their Catholic neighbours and occasionally voiced their Liberal sentiments. But, eventually, their old '98 spirit faded and was replaced in the space of half a century by a complete change of political thought and action.

How My Boxing Career Was Stopped

The interest taken in the Paterson-Monaghan fight brings back to me sad memories of a similar, but much less important, experience in my own young days. It would be thirty-five, maybe forty years ago, when the Star Music Hall, in Church Street, was the Mecca of junior boxing fans, and Saturday evenings brought some exciting bouts. I was something of an amateur myself then and was rather fancied in the club I frequented as a possible bantamweight if I stuck to the game.

How I came to be fancied happened this wise. About six months earlier than the incident I shall describe, I was matched against a pretty tough fighter named Jim Farrell. He could have laid me out in the first round had he wished, but elected to amuse himself with giving me odd taps to let me know what would happen if he got going. During the second round, he obviously left himself open to allow me, at least, one chance to land a blow. I hit him such a whack on the chin that he landed in his own corner, slid down the post, and remained flat on the canvas till his seconds lifted him on to the stool. He swore afterwards the blow I had landed knocked his head against the post and dazed him to such an extent that he couldn't rise to continue.

Probably he was right. In any case, I grabbed my coat and flew for my life. In the club I was hailed as a coming champ. In fact, the members considered I carried a dangerous punch and allowed me to bask in all my glory. Then one Saturday evening the boys hunted me up to tell me the manager of The Star had heard about my progress and arranged a match for me that evening. I wasn't too keen regarding the offer, but the boys would take no excuses and I eventually found myself in The Star dressing room stripped to a pair of trunks. I hadn't the faintest idea who my opponent was to be until I found myself in the ring facing him. I nearly fainted.

Jim Farrell was grinning at me with the ferocity of a hungry wolf. He had resigned from the club immediately after our encounter and gone into professional boxing under the name of Battling Farrell. He looked the battler, too, with his flat nose and cauliflower ears, not to mention his bulging muscles. I explained to the seconds I wasn't feeling too well, and didn't think I could make a show. I am afraid their hearing wasn't perfect.

I had to be pushed out of my corner to meet the referee. He introduced Battler Farrell as the coming champ, and myself as the boy who had yet to be k.o.'d. Farrell winked at me when he heard this, and assured me with one eye that, at least, this part of my reputation was about to terminate.

When the gong sounded, I refused to get to my feet. The stool was whipped from under me, and the round commenced. The Battler hit me where he liked, how he liked, and when he pleased. I made one or two ineffectual attempts to defend myself. He never remained in one place more than a second. The round had barely started when I received a crack on the chin which sent me spinning into my corner, but before I could lie down he tore into me like a wild cat. I was hoping he would step back for a breather to give me the opportunity to slip to the canvas and count myself out. Farrell read my mind and almost lifted me to my feet when my knees sagged. I cursed the day I had ever donned boxing gloves. I managed to keep the referee between us for the rest of the round. In my corner, I appealed to the seconds to throw in the towel. Instead, they threw me into the centre of the ring when the gong sounded for the second round.

With the force of the push my second gave me, I collided with Farrell almost before he had left his corner, and my right elbow nearly cracked his ribs. He went down heavily. I stumbled over him. The audience yelled themselves hoarse with excitement. They actually believed I was fighting back. Only for the referee pulling me back, I would certainly have jumped on top of Farrell to save myself any further trouble. Farrell beat the count, then, with a snarl, came after me. 'After me' are the correct words. I simply hiked it round the ring, with 'The Battler' doing his level best to corner me. When he did manage his point, it was pure murder. Bulldozers, tank-busters, steam-rollers seemed to be coming at me from every angle. When I finally managed to lie down I had no intention of rising any more. The referee fell asleep during the count and the gong sounded at eight.

I lay on happily, hoping the contest would be declared. But no. My seconds pounced on me, planted me on a stool and started work. I pretended semi-consciousness. It didn't work. They emptied the water-bucket over my head and I leaped to my feet with a yell, knocked one of the seconds through the ropes, and charged Farrell almost before the gong sounded before the third round. I went berserk. Farrell, too, lost his temper, and we were both lashing out for all we were worth.

The referee was knocked through the ropes and elected to shout his orders from the ringside. I missed Farrell frequently and grew dizzy as I whirled round and round. I lay down, sat down and was knocked down. Two of my teeth were gone and one eye ceased to function. Farrell's appearance wasn't what you would call handsome either. Then something hit me. I thought the roof of 'The Star' had fallen on top of me and numerous other stars were dropping through the open gap. I tried to hitch myself to one of the stars just as the gable end of the place followed the roof. Then I sailed away aboard a wonderful golden ship into a silvery sea.

Edward Bunting in Belfast

When Edward Bunting arrived in Belfast at an early age he was lucky to be apprenticed to the most outstanding Irish musician outside Dublin. William Ware was a noted organist and musician, but Bunting, young as he was, soon outstripped his master. When his apprenticeship to Ware had finished, in 1790, he travelled the length and breadth of Ireland to collect harp music, a hobby which he eventually made a lifetime study. His research work carried him far into the remote corners of Tyrone and Derry, where he met and talked with the two greatest living exponents of the ancient harp music of their native land. Arthur O'Neill and Denis A. Hempson, both of whom were afflicted with blindness.

Bunting, although born in Armagh of an English father and an Irish mother, became, as did another famous Anglo-Irishman, Jonathan Swift, more Irish than the Irish themselves. When still a child his father died, and Bunting spent some years in Dublin with his brother, who taught music in that town. His brother encouraged young Bunting to take up music as a career, and found him so apt a pupil that he sent him north to give him an opportunity to study under a more proficient master. Bunting was eleven years old when he sat down at the organ of St. Anne's Church in Belfast under the watchful eye of William Ware.

When he returned to Belfast after his meetings with the old harpists, and closely guarding his treasured transcripts of the ancient tunes he had gleaned from the unrehearsed performances of the harpers, he immediately set to work amongst the gentry of the town in an effort to interest them in the ancient music of their country. The Belfast Library, or Society for Promoting Knowledge (now the Linen Hall Library), came to his aid in the persons of Dr. James McDonnell, Henry Joy McCracken and Robert Bradshaw. The Rev. Dr. Hugh O'Donnell, the popular parish priest of St. Mary's, promised to entertain the harpers. A committee was formed and the surviving harpers of Ireland invited to attend a meeting to be held in the Assembly Rooms in Waring Street. Bunting was appointed to take down the notes of the tunes as played by the harpers.

The meeting was a great success, and gave Bunting, although barely nineteen at the time, inspiration to carry on his research work. He was lodging with the McCracken family in their house in High Street since his arrival in the town, and the companionship of Mary McCracken and her brothers, of whom the ill-fated Henry Joy was one, encouraged him to redouble his efforts to place on record for future generations the ancient tunes of his native land.

By 1793, Bunting had collected sufficient airs from the harpers to propose publishing his first volume, but his salary as an assistant organist was too meagre to allow him financial aid. The committee of the Belfast Library, hearing of his difficulties, came to his assistance and, in March of that year, they resolved "that it be recommended to the Society to take said work under patronage; to publish it in London under the name of the Society with a prefatory discourse, allowing the profits derived therefrom to the person who took down the notes, and that a letter be written and signed by the Chairman to Mr. E. Bunting informing him of the Society's intentions".

Bunting accepted the offer, and in April the committee resolved " ... that £50 be transmitted to Mr. Jamison, of London, to be expended in the printing of the Irish music collected by Mr. Bunting, according to the engagement formally made by the Society". The work was published in 1796, but the name of the Society was omitted from the title page. Bunting, some time later, repaid most of the £50 advanced by the library.

Meanwhile, in 1794, Thomas Russell had been appointed librarian of the Society, and Henry Joy McCracken, Robert Simms, John Rabb and Samuel Neilson were serving on the committee, all of them active members of the United Irish movement. Bunting, although neither a member nor even supporter of the group, mixed freely with these young patriots and, when adversity and tragedy came upon them, his friendship never wavered.

When Wolfe Tone visited Belfast for the last time in 1795, he and his friends went on various picnics, when, it is probable, they discussed their future plans for the liberation of their country. Upon one of these occasions, arriving back at the McCracken's home, Bunting joined the company. Persuaded by the McCrackens to entertain their visitors, Bunting played 'The Parting of Friends'. The incident aroused such poignant feeling that Mrs. Wolfe Tone burst into tears and left the room. Tone, Russell and McCracken were fated never to meet again.

In September 1808, Bunting erected the organ for the Second Presbyterian congregation and was appointed organist. He retained this position for ten years. The organ Bunting installed is still in use after an adventurous career. The Second congregation removed from Rosemary Street to its present home, All Souls, Elmwood Avenue, in 1890. In 1912, a new organ was installed, and Bunting's was transported to Newry, where it serves the Presbyterian church in which John Mitchel's father at one time officiated.

Bunting's second volume of Irish airs was published in 1809, his first attempt bringing in little profit. Some years earlier, Thomas Moore and his friend, Sir John Stevenson, had published a volume of seventeen Irish airs, eleven of them having been collected by Bunting. The public assumed that Moore was the author. He made no attempt to correct this. It was just too bad that copyright law did not exist at the time.

Bunting, who had developed into a fashionable 'man-about-town', met and became attached to a Miss Chapman, who resided in a shop owned by her mother in Curtis Street, Belfast. He married this lady in 1819 and changed his habits before it became too late. Finally, he moved to Dublin some time after his marriage, and was soon a popular figure in Dublin society. He still corresponded with the McCrackens, and continued to do so till his death.

In 1840, he published his last and finest work, a collection of 150 ancient Irish airs, of which 120 were published for the first time. The book was dedicated to the young Queen Victoria, which reveals the fact that Bunting was now admitted into the inner circle of Dublin aristocracy.

He died in 1843, but it was some years later before his real value as a contributor to the ancient music of Ireland was recognised. Thomas Moore's personality and popularity had overshadowed Bunting during his lifetime, but eventually his lifework as a collector of ancient Irish airs was recorded in the annals of Irish music, to be remembered for all time by future generations of Irish people.

I Have Faith in Ireland

A new year has dawned for Ireland. What it may bring forth to enrich the country is surely not alone the wish but the prayer of every Irish man and woman.

Up here in the six counties, we are facing problems that will not be easily overcome. Probably you in the south will have similar troubles to keep your minds occupied and your politicians worried. Although I am neither a politician nor a prophet, I have a feeling deep down in my heart that north and south are drawing nearer to an understanding of each other that has never happened in the troubled history of our country since the Plantation days.

I believe in the ultimate happiness of Ireland because I am an Irishman with an Irishman's love for his fatherland.

If, as history records, my ancestors crossed the narrow channel which separated Ulster from their Scottish home some three hundred years ago, and settled in County Down to the disgust and disadvantage of the native Irish, am I to blame if they looked on the land with approval and decided that this was to be theirs and their children's home for all time?

For three hundred years, my forbears have been laid to rest beneath an ancient round tower in the grounds of the Presbyterian church of Drumbo, Co. Down. How an Irish round tower managed to become planted in a Presbyterian cemetery is a fact I have no wish to argue upon. There is a possibility it was there before we formed the Drumbo congregation. They couldn't have transported it from Fifeshire, because, so far as I recollect, Scotland possesses no round towers.

Still, my father was always very proud of that round tower, and it would have been foolhardy for any visitor to question their right of ownership.

The centuries living on Irish soil has salted our blood with a kinship that cleaves to every mountain, glen and wooded valley in this beautiful northland, and we do not take kindly to any who question our right of inheritance.

Even the fact that five generations of my family were connected with Orangeism, and I myself have been Worshipful Master of an Independent Orange lodge, does not make me any less of an Irishman than a member of the Hibernian Order or that of the Knights of Columbanus.

The religious and political differences which affect our people carry a similarity to problems which confront other nations scattered all over the globe. We remain floundering around, living in the past, cautious as to the future.

During my early childhood days, living in the industrial quarters of Belfast, I occasionally managed an excursion into the country or an hour or two at the seaside.

I can recollect to this day how my face would be pressed against the carriage window and my childish mind astounded that such beauty could exist so near to my home and be actually part of the land that gave me birth. Since then, I have travelled and soldiered in many lands but I have yet to discover any country that could rouse similar passions in my breast.

When I first climbed Slieve Donard mountain, in the Mournes, and looked down on the beautiful Kingdom of Mourne, then cast my gaze across Carlingford Lough into Omeath, I could visualise no border, just a great affection in my heart for my country that neither sectarian nor political animosities could ever smother.

If it were possible to transport every individual Irishman to such a corner of the land, the solution of Ireland's troubles would be settled for all time.

I remember one of my brothers who was serving in the 36th Ulster Division during World War I, and who adopted an extraordinary antipathy towards all his southern countrymen, coming out of the Battle of Messines Ridge, where the two Irish divisions went into action side by side, with a fierce admiration for the courage and comradeship of the Connacht men that remained with him through all the troubles that followed.

On the face of it, one is almost forced to believe that Ireland can never become a unified country. This is rubbish. A year could see the whole edifice of the border crumble. The two governments are drawing nearer to that so-called Utopian dream every year of their existence.

The Lough Erne Drainage Scheme and the GNR agreement are only two examples of the friendly understanding which has grown up of late between the two states.

The six counties still remain a cultural part of the Irish nation, despite their thirty-year separation. Their drama, poetry, literature and music have yet to be influenced by political turmoil or the economic agreements with the Westminster government.

A community does not relinquish its traditions, customs, literature and speech because of an internal political quarrel within the nation. Bullets and party bitterness may separate communities for a generation, but never for all time.

A couple of months ago the Belfast Centre of the Irish PEN discussed a number of flaws in the constitution of the club detrimental to the feelings of many northern members. There was a flare up of tempers and it was almost decided to separate from the Dublin centre, when a suggestion was made that delegates be appointed to talk matters over with the southern centre. A conference lasting a couple of hours revealed how easily such differences could be settled without using an atom bomb.

King Cricket Once Again

With the cricket season on its way, followers of the game are polishing up their bats. But I wonder how many fans have ever considered the origin of the game, or even when it first became popular, or who may have been the earliest wielder of the bat?

Cricket, in some rude form, dates back to the 13th century. That is, our ancestors hit the ball with a club and made a run. In the early 18th century the bat, or club, had a very thin handle, but thickened and curved like a hockey stick at the end.

There were four or five fielders plus the bowler. Two upright sticks were used instead of three. The sticks were a foot high and the same apart, with another stick as bail. But they used only one set of stumps in those days. About 1777, the third stick was added, and the bowling changed to overhand, or 'throwing' as it was called for many years.

Towards the end of the 18th century, the two sets of stumps were brought into play, although there were still no more than half a dozen fielders. For instance, in 1792 Eton played the MCC with four men to field on either side.

During 1820, a form of rules was drawn up in which the batsman was 'out' if the ball was struck up and he wilfully took another swipe.

Another rule explained that if any person stopped the ball with his hat, the ball was considered dead, and the opposing side received five runs added to their score.

The earliest record I can find of cricket being played in Belfast is 1840, when the Belfast Cricket Club occupied a pitch somewhere convenient to what is now the Corporation Electricity Offices, at Laganbank Road.

The club was established "for the purpose of affording young men an opportunity of partaking in the healthful, noble game of cricket". The club consisted of ordinary and honorary members, who met "for exercise" on Monday, Wednesday, Thursday and Friday evenings, and on Tuesday, Thursday and Saturday mornings—at 6 am.

Among the patrons were the Marquis of Donegall, Lord Lurgan, and R. B. Blakiston-Houston. Members wore flat-topped hats at practice and top-hats at matches.

Nearest record to the above, so far as I can discover, is a cricket club established at Ormeau in 1858. The members possessed a clubhouse at that time, and the pitch was probably that on which North of Ireland Cricket Club began to function, because in 1861 there is no doubt that North had commenced a career which continues till the present day.

Later—I think round about the '70s— Cliftonville Cricket Club secured a pitch in that district and the game really began to take root in Belfast.

Porter of Greyabbey

On a warm, sunny day in the month of July 1798, a scaffold was erected between the manse and the Presbyterian Meeting House at Greyabbey, County Down. To this place, with pinioned arms, they hurried the Rev. James Porter, of the Greyabbey congregation, and hanged him till life gave out. It was the climax to a long standing feud between the reverend gentleman and the Londonderry family.

The rebellion had already been crushed and McCracken, Munro and the other leaders executed. Jimmy Hope, Orr and a few stalwarts of the movement had managed to escape, some to the mountains, others to America. Those who remained were hunted from pillar to post until exhaustion or the paid informer cornered them, and they inevitably paid the penalty.

Why Porter was not charged with treason until some weeks after the rebellion had been crushed cannot be easily explained. Probably the Castle authorities had no particular anxiety to clash with the Presbyterians as a body. Most of their clergy were behind prison bars, and it was far from the Castle's policy to antagonise the General Assembly.

Be that as it may, the Rev. Porter had travelled far beyond the pale of leniency. Lord Londonderry had a score to settle with the reverend gentleman, and My Lord's son, Castlereagh, possessed the power and position to see the score was levelled up. Porter had taken no active part in the rebellion, neither was he a sworn United man, so the difficulty was to fabricate a suitable charge.

With dozens of paid government emissaries sneaking around the countryside, they eventually established a method of involving Porter into active participation in the troubles. He was charged with intercepting dispatches prior to the battle of Saintfield, in which the royalist forces were defeated. To prove this charge was merely a matter of arrangement with the suitable witnesses. It may have been coincidence that Lord Londonderry's land steward was the presiding magistrate. Porter was found guilty and executed without delay, and in the most brutal fashion.

Although a Donegal man and educated in Glasgow, Porter's first call to the ministry came from the Greyabbey congregation. The congregation, though numerous, was by no mean wealthy, as most of the landed gentry belonged to the established church. Still as a cultured and learned divine, his scientific and classical attainments had reached such a high standard that even the Londonderry family accepted him as an equal, and allowed their children to attend his lectures.

Like many of his ministerial brethren of the General Assembly of that day, he held pronounced liberal opinions which soon brought him into conflict with the landed gentry of the neighbourhood. He was rash with his pen, frank in speech and imbued with a courage which, in those days, earned little in return except persecution and imprisonment. He lashed out with his pen at all and sundry whom he considered enemies of his people, but his pet aversions were the two most powerful landowners of the surrounding countryside, the Lords Londonderry and Downshire.

Porter was a family man. At the time of his execution, he had six daughters and two sons. This alone, if his character had been other than it was, should have made him a docile and subservient retainer of the land squires. His pamphlets were open attacks on the privileged class, his sermons powerful pleas for democratic government, free speech and the liberties of the people.

When his tragic fate overtook him in 1798, he had not yet attained middle age, was married eighteen years, and had been in the ministry less than fourteen years. After his execution, an attempt was made in the Assembly to deprive his widow of the usual pension which was settled upon the family of a deceased minister. It is to the credit of the General Assembly of the day that the motion was defeated, and Porter's family was, to some extent, saved from absolute poverty.

The majority of the Rev. Porter's daughters married Presbyterian ministers. His two sons emigrated to America after the execution of their father. Both became lawyers. One of the brothers eventually rose to the status of a judge in the high court and was later elected to represent his state in the Senate of the United States.

Some years ago, whilst in the neighbourhood of Kircubbin, I came across a female descendant of the Porter family. I was ushered into the sitting-room of her home and proudly shown an oil painting of the Rev. Porter in clerical garb. I discovered some time later that the late Francis Joseph Bigger had visited the lady on a previous occasion and been given permission to have the painting photographed in case the picture should be destroyed or lost to prosperity.

The Rev. Porter's remains were laid to rest in the cemetery adjoining the old abbey. A plain stone slab marks the grave to record his name and date of death. It is in good preservation. The congregation still functions to perpetuate the memory and sacrifice of one of the early pastors.

Teams of the Good Old Days

It is a pity no student of sport has attempted to write a history of football in Ulster. When I was a child, all the present senior teams were in existence, at least, in Belfast. Previous to that, there were many popular teams, now forgotten.

There were Limavady, Magherafelt, Oldpark, Moyola, Ulster and Queen's Island. The two last appeared later as Ulster Rangers, but Queen's Island resumed their original title. This was in 1882. There were a few other teams in senior football whose names have passed into oblivion.

Distillery came into the picture on February 7th 1881, when it made its debut in the Irish Challenge Cup, meeting Knock in the first round. And received a knock, too, for Knock defeated them by eleven goals to nil. But they knew how to take a licking without tears and continued to play up

Broadway direction until they made good.

By 1887, football had a steady grip on the Belfast public. Glentoran were now functioning, and on October 8th of that year Cliftonville gave them a shock by trouncing them 6-0. But the Reds were veterans even at that time. Then Ulster, another veteran combination, playing at Ballynafeigh, beat them four to one in November.

In the same year, some of our combinations were challenging a number of crack English teams. On October 1st, Cliftonville beat Clitheroe (Lancashire) by no less than ten goals to nil, and followed this up by a narrow win over Airdrieonians. Distillery, travelling to Blackburn, were unlucky to be defeated by the odd goal in three.

On November 7th, Distillery met a crack English team called Wilton in the second round of the English Cup. This combination had already defeated Blackburn and Everton. The local team went down with colours flying, although licked by four goals to two. Preston North End paid Distillery a visit shortly after this, and the local team again admitted defeat by three to one.

Linfield Athletic, not more than a few months in senior football, played the Highland Light Infantry to a draw of two each, and then scored a sensational five to three victory over the veteran Ulster combination.

The team in 1887—McCracken, Clarke, J. Torrens, McKeown, Sharpe, Peyton, S. Torrens, R. Torrens, Calvert and McCorry.

Their reserve team didn't do well during the same year, for Milltown piled up seven goals to nil against them at their Linfield pitch.

On January 5th 1887, Ireland travelled to Sheffield to meet the pick of English football in an international match. According to the press "an immense concourse gathered to watch the teams battle for the Triple Crown". There were 6,000 spectators. England won by seven goals to nil. Still, the Irish team gives one an idea of the various clubs functioning at the time: Goal, Gillespie (Hertford); backs, Fox (Ulster) and F. Browne (Cliftonville); half-backs, Rosbotham (Cliftonville), Allen (Limavady), and Crone (Distillery); left wing, M. M. Browns (Limavady) and Leslie (YMCA); centre, Gibb (Wellington Park, capt.); right wing, Small (Clarence) and Stanfield (Distillery).

On February 19th, they travelled to Hampden Park, Glasgow, to meet Scotland. J. Peden (Linfield) replaced one of the players, but it was of no avail. Scotland won by four to one before 3,000 spectators. Back in Belfast, practically the same combination met Wales at Ulster's ground in Ballynafeigh. On this occasion, before 5,000 fan, we escaped the Wooden Spoon by defeating the visitors by four to one.

The year 1887 is a long way off, and many clubs and their players have passed into history. Still, it is well to remember the pioneers of those days, when there was little to make at the game except the appreciation of the club's supporters.

The Belfast Man

Francis Davis, the poet, who will always be remembered as 'The Belfast Man', was neither born in the city nor yet were his parents in any way connected with the north. Davis, in fact, was born in Ballincollig, Co. Cork, in 1810. His parents travelled north when the child was barely three years old and settled in Hillsborough, County Down. What induced the Davis family to migrate to Ulster, and, stranger still, settle in Hillsborough, above all places remains a mystery. The Downshire family were lords of the manor in this portion of Down, and owned or controlled everything but the souls of their tenants. The Davis family were Catholics and how they managed to practice their faith in their new surroundings we can only surmise.

There was a school in Hillsborough village which, with Lord Downshire's patronage taught the poorer tenants' children an elementary approach to English. To this school, at the age of seven, came young Davis. His mother, who was not illiterate, had done her best to instruct Francis in the simpler forms of spelling and grammar, and she had succeeded to such an extent that the old be-whiskered master made the lad a proud exhibit of his own tuition when My Lord and Lady paid their periodical visits. It was considered by many in those days as a danger to society to educate working-class children, and Francis was luckier than most of his fellows in surviving three years before being sent out to earn his own livelihood at the age of ten years. And so Francis arrived in Belfast about 1820, to learn the art of weaving.

The industrial revolution was in its infancy and the Mulhollands had yet to introduce the power loom into their factory in Belfast. Most of the weaving fraternity in the town lived in and around Brown Square and Peter's Hill, but there were others who plied their calling in the neighbourhood of Smithfield in close proximity to St. Mary's Chapel. It was probably here that young Francis learned his trade. Jimmy Hope, discovering that his zealous efforts to keep alive the cause he held so dear to his heart was of no further avail, had by this time settled at Peter's Hill with his fellow-weavers. Whether young Davis ever came under the influence of the indomitable insurgent leader I have never been able to discover, yet I cannot believe these two were unknown to each other. Their lives, spent in the service of the downtrodden, were almost identical.

It was during the early of Davis's literary career, when his contributions to the *Nation* newspaper were attracting attention, that he was continuously being referred to as 'The Belfast Man', so that readers would not confuse his efforts with that of his contemporary Protestant poet, Thomas Davis, of the Young Ireland movement. Francis Davis, published his first volume of poetry, *Lispings of the Lagan*, in 1844. These were simple, charming lays, springing from the heartbeats of an artisan whose slavish toil at the loom almost smothered the yearning for beauty and the desire for expression which inevitably comes to each of us whatever our calling or station in life.

There were others of his class in his neighbourhood striving for similar recognition. Poor Andrew MacKenzie, the Shankill labourer-poet, had died through neglect a few years previously, and Edward Sloan, another Belfast labouring man was making ineffectual attempts to have his poems accepted for publication, which he eventually accomplished ten years later. In Ballyclare, another weaver poet, Thomas Beggs, who had published no less than seven volumes, was nearing his end, whilst in Ballymena, David Herbison, a fellow-craftsman of the loom, was issuing his fifth volume. Davis was in good company.

A London newspaper, criticising Davis's early poems in the *Nation*, remarked: "Davis's idea of liberty and slavery extend no further than the shores of his own country." To this he replied: "My ideas of liberty and slavery, in short, my whole political creed may be reduced to two bare words—Human Liberty."

In 1847, he published *Poems and Songs*. Still, not satisfied with an output of mere verse, Davis tried his hand at publishing prose and, in 1850, he edited his own magazine, *The Belfastman's Journal*. He failed to get sufficient backing and the venture failed, but his reputation as a writer brought him recognition at a dinner held in his honour by a number of cultured Belfast citizens. Amongst the more liberal-minded gentry of the town he was treated as an equal. The Earl of Belfast, Lieut. Calder and Dr. Malcolm, prominent reformers of a century ago in Belfast, sought his company and advice.

In 1855, he returned to his old love, and published a long poem, entitled 'Belfast: The City and the Man'. Up till now his work had been published in Belfast, but London was taking notice of this weaver-poet and his next effort, again a long poem, 'The Tablet of Shadows', was accepted by a London publishing house. Two years later another long poem, 'Leaves from our Cypress and our Oak', received a London hallmark. Then Davis went back to prose and published in Belfast a rather disjointed essay, 'Rambles and Gossip Along Highways and Byways Round Belfast'. This work resembled a travelogue extending from the White Linen Hall to Malone, by way of Stranmillis.

He had reached his fifty-sixth year by now, and almost fifty years of manual labour and literary activities combined sapped all his energy. To add to this, he had not alone conquered the French language, but also acquired an elementary knowledge of Greek and Latin.

Davis's final contribution to the literature of his native land was published in 1877, under the title of *Earlier and Later Leaves*, with an introductory essay on the author by the Rev. Columban O'Grady OP, Belfast. This was a selection from his former volumes and covered many pages.

Davis was an old man now, unable to continue his labour as a weaver, worn out and neglected by those he had striven all his life to inspire towards a higher and nobler standard. Father O'Grady made a powerful appeal to the public not to allow Davis's contribution to Irish literature to go unrewarded and his life to finish in poverty and shameless neglect. The response to this appeal was soon apparent when the government of the day settled a civil pension of £50 per annum upon Davis, which meant his remaining years were spent, to some extent, in comfort and security.

Davis passed away in 1885, and was laid to rest in Milltown cemetery, where a monument was erected to his memory.

Francis Davis may well be remembered as 'The Belfast Man', for to this weaver-poet the town of his adoption was the centre of his inspiration. No word ever crept into his writings that would harm or disparage his home town. His steadfast loyalty was appreciated even by those who disagreed with his political and religious principles. He cuddled the Divis mountain to his heart, and the soft lilt of his song flowed in rhythm with the Lagan waters by whose banks he was wont to stroll.

The Theatre in Older Belfast

There is no longer any doubt that Belfast has become theatre-minded. The two repertory theatres in the city are attracting full houses nightly, and the Opera House, when it chooses to book drama or ballet for the entertainment of its patrons, rarely misplaces its faith in the general public's regard for 'the play'. The amateur dramatic societies, which are ever on the increase, are a sure sign that the theatre has regained much of the ground it undoubtedly lost between the two great wars.

I can well remember the state of local drama, some thirty years ago, when the Ulster Literary Theatre was at its lowest ebb. They tried every type of play in an attempt to interest the public, but it proved an impossible task at the time. The cinema had swamped the theatre, both commercial and repertory. Few of us ever dreamed it would regain the affection of the public in the space of a generation.

Yet tradition dies hard, and Belfast had reason to be proud of its theatrical history, not to the same extent as London or Dublin, but for a town of small beginnings there had been many gallant ventures to establish a permanent theatre in the town from its earliest days.

The O'Neills often engaged strolling players to perform in their castles, and it is to the credit of a number of the more cultured Planter families that they, too, encouraged the art to survive the troubled years of northern history.

The first recorded attempt to establish a theatre in Belfast was in the year 1740. The proprietor rented an extensive hayloft at the rear of Castle Place, and, with the help of a few artisans, soon had a fairly decent stage and auditorium erected. Large posters flooded the town with the news of the first performance of *The School for Lovers*.

Some years later, in 1754, Charles Lewis, of Covent Garden, rented a tavern in Ann Street and constructed it into a makeshift theatre, giving it the name of 'The Vaults Theatre'. It was opened on the 18th November, 1754, with a tragedy called *The Fair Penitent*. Lewis moved on to Derry on March 14th 1755. The prices of admission were: pit, 2s 2d; gallery 1s 1d.

On the 28th February 1766, "a new ballad farce, never performed on any stage before, and entitled *The Humours of Belfast*, with an occasion prologue, written by a gentleman of this place", received a tumultuous reception.

Another venture, this time a small wooden construction erected near the Millgate, close to the present Chapel Lane, was opened by a Mr. Ryder about 1770. This particular theatre only lasted four months, when Mr. Ryder left the town to take over the management of the famous Smock Alley Theatre in Dublin.

The Millgate Theatre was brought into use occasionally by visiting companies, but was considered a disgrace to drama and eventually give place to a new theatre owned by Myrton Hamilton and managed by Michael Atkins, in Ann Street.

The premises were opened to the public on the 23rd October 1778. The play for that evening was entitled *Rule a Wife and Have a Wife*, written by no less a person than the famous David Garrick.

Hamilton and Atkins worked the Ann Street jointly for four-and-a-half years before they separated, Atkins starting a new venture alone in Rosemary Street. The Ann Street Theatre gradually lost its audience and finally disappeared as a place of entertainment.

On the other hand, Atkins became a popular manager and his Rosemary Street house became a fashionable resort for the gentry of Belfast. It was in this theatre that Mrs. Sarah Siddons occupied the stage for three weeks in 1785.

Michael Atkins now had the field to himself and seemed to have placed the town on the map regarding the theatre world. The Rosemary Street Theatre being a wooden construction, seating less than 400 people, Atkins decided to build a larger building and more durable. In February 1793, the predecessor of the old Theatre Royal was opened to the public.

The most renowned actors of the period appeared upon the boards of the new theatre in Arthur Street. Mrs. Siddons visited the theatre twice, in 1802 and 1805. Her brother John Phillip Kemble, performed here in 1809, to be followed by the youngest brother, Charles Kemble, in 1812. The great Edmund Kean played Richard III in 1817. He made a return visit seven years later when gas had been introduced into the theatre for illumination.

Another famous actor, William Charles Macready, appeared in Belfast on many occasions between 1824 and 1850. The theatre fell into some ill repute after this and the local clergy declaimed against drama to such an extent that the establishment was compelled to close its doors, until J. F. Warden took up the management in 1863 and brought it back to prosperity.

The Arthur Street Theatre having served its purpose for nearly eighty years, was demolished in 1871 and a new home of drama took its place on September 25th of the same year. This theatre was completely destroyed by fire on June 8th 1881. J.F. Warden again rebuilt the theatre and opened it to the public on the 22nd December in the same year. Barry Sullivan's company gave the first performance in the new Theatre Royal before a distinguished audience, and Mr. Walden received a tremendous reception when he was called before the curtain to make a speech.

During the following years, the theatre welcomed many great figures and made theatrical history. Henry Irving, the Batemans, the Comptons, the Carl Rosa and D'Oyley Carte Opera Companies and, later, F.R. Benson and Forbes Robertson.

After the Opera House was built in the late '90s, the old Theatre Royal was generally the home of melodrama and Easter pantomimes, but I still recollect that neither Benson or Forbes Robertson would change their theatre, although Irving, Compton and the Terrys did. I don't remember Martin Harvey ever playing in the Theatre Royal although I saw him twice in the Opera House.

After a period of one hundred and twenty-three years, the Arthur Street venue was closed down finally as a theatre and re-opened as the Royal Cinema on December 29th 1916.

The Worker as Writer

Seekers after knowledge are not necessarily all drawn from the educated classes, although the majority of our greatest men of letters are known to have acquired an early opportunity to attain a degree of learning withheld from the manual worker. Universities can teach you the philosophy of life before you have experienced the actual fact of living. Most workers, especially those of a few generations back, were already caught up in the maelstrom of life years before their minds could shape a thought as to why this or that should be.

Learning was practically forbidden to the manual worker until the second half of last century. To be a good labourer was considered the proper achievement for the worker; to be a good scholar was a dangerous asset. The plough and the spade and the hammer were sufficient for his needs. The Church thought otherwise and built schools, but these were frowned upon by the landed gentry. In the province of Ulster these schools were, accordingly, few and far between.

Outside the Church schools, there was little incentive for the worker to educate himself. When, about the middle of the 19th century, the skilled workmen thought it expedient to form themselves into mutual help groups, the authorities realised that only force could deprive these people of their ambitions. When force failed, they tried ridicule and persecution.

Before industrialism drove the land worker into the slums and pest houses of the north-eastern town of the province, there were around the country individual members of the working-class population who had self-educated themselves to a standard that caused their fellows to respect and honour them. Among these were Jimmy Hope of Templepatrick; James Orr of Ballycarry, and James Campbell of Larne. All were weavers and poets of no mean order.

The leaders of the United Irish Society, all of whom were drawn from middle-class social life, realised that without these men in their ranks there could be no approach to the mass of the people. Hope, Orr, and Campbell were never leaders of the movement, but they inspired in the breasts of their fellows an ambition to be free men and, more important still, to be intelligent free men.

Weavers in the province in those days were the élite of manual workers. Illiteracy was the common lot amongst both farm workers and townsmen alike. Here and there about the province, an individual worker would strive to conquer the written word. The weavers were the pioneers of this new and revolutionary movement amongst the people. Beggs of Glenwherry; Porter of Monyslan, Herbinson of Ballymena; Francis Davis of Belfast, added volumes of poetry and philosophy to the workers library.

Then machinery arrived to oust the handloom weaver, and the power-loom factories soon crushed the spirit of learning out of the hearts of these men. Another type of worker sprang up to carry on the tradition. John Close of Ewart's factory, and Adam Lynn of Cullybackey, two linen workers, put into verse the aspirations of the spinner and weaver.

During the Crimean War, a Belfast labourer, Edward Sloan, published a volume which brought him more abuse than praise from the critics of the day. He thundered out an anti-war poem which shocked the very souls of the war-mongers of the period, revealing in strong, virile lines the cruelty and misery of the Crimean strife. In later days, another manual workers of no particular calling, Oliver Porter of Hillsborough, issued a volume of poems whilst living in London. He later emigrated to California, and the last I heard of Porter, from a Sandy Row relative, was that he had been elected president of the San Pedro Writers' Club.

Navvying is not a profession in which one can lie back and muse on the beauty of Nature. The life is too raw and the work is too cruel to rouse in a man's breast a desire to dream. Yet, Patrick Magill, a Donegal farm labourer, who later became a navvy, told the navvyman's story in prose and verse. It wasn't until Magill ceased his connection with the navvy that his popularity as a writer faded.

Dock workers, too, have little time and less inclination to ornament their working days with garlands of roses. The noise and bustle of loading and unloading ships gives the docker about as much leisure to breathe as it does to ruminate on the pleasant things of life. I remember, thirty years ago, a Belfast docker, Mic Nolan, between spells in the stokehole and at the docks, passing on some fine verses to our local paper. Another docker, whose name I have forgotten, lived on the Old Lodge Road about twenty years ago, and produced poetry of an exceptionally high standard. A few years ago, I met another docker, living in the Ardoyne district, who not alone had literary talent but also dabbled with the brush and used his leisure hours painting.

Amongst the manual workers with whom I have had occasion to mix, I should say that woodworkers would rank the highest in intelligence and craftsmanship. Few were of a literary bend of mind. One, Francis Boal of Comber, did issue a book during the early years of the last century. But they do make good politicians.

Printers, whose trade makes it imperative to possess a knowledge of English, rarely shine as writers, which fact is, to say the least, extraordinary. Curiously enough, too, journeymen painters rarely develop the art of picture-making, although their craft leads them to invent colour schemes which could be both original and pleasing on canvas. Still, Tommy Henderson MP and Joseph Tomelty were among both journeymen painters at one time.

Flax-dressers, or hecklers as they are better known, have supplied Stormont with two very prominent members in the past but, so far as my research work has gone, they have added nothing to the literature of the province. This is a pity because, in the early days, they had a custom in the mills amongst that fraternity which tended to encourage interest in writing.

In the hecklers room, where the men worked at benches, one 'berth' was set aside for the 'Reader'. This man instead of working at his trade, read the morning newspapers to his comrades. He was at no loss, as his share of the work was covered by the rest of his mates. When occasion arose, an open discussion would be carried on in regard to the definition of a particular word in English. I am not sure whether a dictionary was ever produced to settle the argument.

Perhaps an abler pen than mine will some day revive the memory of our forgotten working-men writers.

Time Will Heal the Breach

I have been thinking of late what kind of an impression we six-counties' folk are making on the British and American tourists who visit this part of Ireland. As a community, I am fairly certain we puzzle most visitors to our shores.

Our speech is an uncertain variety of Scottish, English and Irish words, which have almost to be translated to be understood. Yet this peculiar exclusiveness to the north-eastern counties of Ireland carries romance and sentiment as to its origin.

A great failing many northerners have is our utter lack of interest in the history and legends attached to almost every strip of land in the north. The fault, perhaps, doesn't lie with the people, but with the government.

They have yet to produce a schoolbook giving the reader an outline of northern history. A country without history is somewhat like a man without a name; he is born, lives, dies and is forgotten.

How many northerners have ever considered the value of their heritage, the traditions which surround every village and townland of the six counties; the ancient legends which were already hoary with age when the history of man was first written. But to say that we do not cherish these would be a lie.

But history alone cannot make a land worthy of sacrifice. If a people can only point to war as a monument of their existence, it is of little matter to mankind if they be conquered and scattered. If they have not inspired civilisation with their knowledge and institutions they have not earned their freedom.

Yet who can deny this Ulster of ours has given as great a contribution as similar regions to the knowledge of mankind?

We have to remember that, when the continent of Europe was still peopled with warlike and pagan nations, it was from the shores of Belfast Lough the first pioneers of the new Christian civilisation went forth to enrich the world with their learning and martyrdom.

My earliest recollection of what feelings were towards my native land was an intense pride in being born an Irishman. Whether this emotion was inherited, or merely developed from a natural instinct, is beside the point. It has always been there, and looks like remaining for all time.

My ancestors came to Ulster to avoid persecution because of their Covenanting principles. Drumbo, where they settled, was one of the first Presbyterian communities in Co. Down. Antrim and Down have many such settlements.

Still, that is all ancient history. I live in my own time. I am not one of those people who believe that Ireland will remain a sliced-up country for all time. No artificial border can split a nation in two by merely drawing a line of demarcation.

It may take a few generations to heal the breach. But, when the ultimate fate of a whole people depends on a solution, that solution will arrive in one form or another.

There is something fundamentally wrong with a country that could support a population of 8,000,000 people a hundred years ago, which today can barely sustain half that number. Three of my boys left home to settle abroad. The fact that they are doing well in their new surroundings is no compensation to me for the loss of their companionship in the home country.

This is 1955.

Time can heal all the sores and tribulations of a disrupted people, and intelligent reasoning and understanding of each other's shortcomings guide us along a path which can alone lead to a happy and prosperous nation.

Ulster Working-men Poets

Studying the literature of Ulster from the end of the 18th century up till the present day, one is struck by the large numbers of working-class writers who have contributed not a little towards that branch of literature which is held by scholars to be "the art of expressing in melodious words the thoughts which are the creations of feelings and imagination".

In many collections and anthologies of Anglo-Irish poetry, it has been the common practice practically to ignore all northern poets who have contributed to the vast volume of national verse. For this reason, many of our Ulster poets have gone into oblivion. Judging from the amount of volumes published in Ulster during the nineteenth and present century, it is doubtful whether any of the other three provinces can outpoint our people in their love of poetry.

Weaving, which has been the most important industry north of the Boyne for centuries, has supplied the majority of our working-class poets, and when you consider the state of education, the conditions under which the commoner people must certainly have laboured, it reflects great credit on the capacity for acquiring knowledge with which the weaving fraternity seems to have been endowed.

The advent of the worker into Ulster literature began in the latter part of the 18th century with the rise of the United Irishmen. Three Ulster poets who took a prominent part in the movement are still remembered—James Hope of Templepatrick, James Orr of Ballycarry, and James Campbell of Larne. Much of their work was composed of patriotic verse. Both Hope and Orr were active at the Battle of Antrim on the rebel side. Hope, who lived the latter part of his life at Peter's Hill, Belfast, is buried at Mallusk, on the road to Templepatrick. Orr has a fine Masonic tomb erected to his memory in Ballycarry old graveyard. Campbell's grave is unknown.

Of the three, James Orr was probably the more outstanding, as two volumes of his verse were published in the early years of the last century. One of his poems, 'The Irishman', is still included in many Irish anthologies, but his finest contribution to Ulster verse, in my opinion, is that voiced in his 'Prayer', written upon the eve of the Battle of Antrim.

> Let not this frame, whose fleshless bones
>   These summer's suns may bleach,
> Lie withering long; nor, while it stands,
>   The hand of pillage stretch.
> But in the victory or the rout,
>   In glory, or in gall,
> May moderation mark my power,
>   And fortitude my fall.

Hugh Porter of Moneyslan, who owing to ill health lived in great poverty with his young family, was assisted by a number of gentlemen to publish a volume of dialect verse in 1810. Another weaver poet, Andrew MacKenzie, who was evicted from his home in Ballywalter and came to reside at Peter's Hill, published a volume about the same time. MacKenzie has a monument erected to his memory in Shankill graveyard. A carpenter of Comber, Francis Boal, also came into prominence about this time with *County Down Songs*.

During the first half of the last century, Ulster weaver poets practically monopolised the literary sky. Thomas Beggs of Glenwherry, has no less than six volumes of verse to his credit. He died at Ballyclare in 1847. David Herbison of Ballymena was the author of five volumes. Herbison was afflicted with blindness at three years of age, migrated to Canada at 27, returned to Ireland, and died at Ballymena in 1880.

At the same time as Herbison was writing, there lived in Falls Road a Belfast weaver named Francis Davis. Davis was not only the author of six volumes of verse, but he also edited a local magazine—*The Belfastman's Journal*— and eventually became one of the librarians at Queen's College, now Queen's University. Perhaps the most outstanding achievement of Davis' career was the fact the government of the day endowed him with a civil pension of £50 per annum as a reward for his cultural activities. He died in 1885 and was laid to rest in Milltown cemetery.

With the passing of the hand-loom into power-loom weaving, the traditional urge of the weaver to express himself in verse was lost, yet not inevitably lost, for in 1879 a linen-lapper, John Close, who, I believe, worked in Ewart's Mill, produced *Echoes Of The Valley*. Some 30 years later another linen worker, Adam Lynn of Cullybackey, issued a volume of verse in Co. Antrim dialect.

An iron moulder, Edward Sloan, who lived in Lagan Village, which was situated on the Ravenhill Road, but is now demolished, published a volume in 1854 with the assistance of a member of the Sharman-Crawford family. These poems are of a fairly high standard and have one particular poem included, entitled 'War', written during the Crimean struggle which occurred exactly one hundred years ago. Here are two stanzas from the piece:

> 'Tis the parent of taxation,
> Fleecing every thriving nation—
> Blasting commerce—ruination
>   In its track.
> 'Tis the sweeping simoom's power,
> Scathing fruit, and plant, and flower,
> Ripening fields, and lovely bower
>   With its blast.

Another artisan, this time a painter, Oliver Porter, who, like myself, was born in Sandy Row, issued a volume of poems in London under 50 years ago, and added another collection a few years back in San Pedro, California, to which he emigrated about 40 years ago. Porter, who still resides in California, was president of the San Pedro Writers' Guild for many years, and no later than this carried off the premier prize for the best poem of the year.

Strange, that in a region where agricultural workers are also numerous, few have joined the ranks of their artisan brothers in revealing their thoughts in verse. But Armagh has supplied the want in W.J. Steenson, a farm labourer, in a volume, *The Apple Blossom and Other Poems*, published in 1923. Steenson I last heard of as having migrated to England during a harvest.

Two policemen have contributed volumes to Ulster poetry—Benjamin Lyness, *Orange and Love Poems*, in 1842, printed in Belfast, and David Blair Watson, an RUC constable, who is still serving. Watson, who hails from Ballymena, has produced two volumes. His last volume, printed in Belfast, bears the title *Rhymes of a Beatman* and contains some impressive lines:

> High from a restless, slumbering fire
> Dark passions' flames leap, and devour
> Reason; God grant me in this hour,
> Clean thoughts, like wings,
> That I may rise on them to higher
>   And nobler things.

These working-class poets I have mentioned are picked at random from a host of versifiers, most from Down and Antrim, who toiled at their looms and machines and ploughs, lived amongst their own people, and are now barely remembered. Yet, in their own lifetime, they made an impression on the literature of their native province and for this alone they deserve something more than oblivion.

Adventures in Search of Work

When I look back over many years of manual work in various jobs in factory, workshop, mill, shipyard and on the highways, I still retain a belief in the dignity of labour. There have been occasions when lean times, unemployment or, worse still, the lack of appreciation of one's worth as a unit of the labour force, tends to rouse a bitterness of one's soul that breeds discontent against your fellow man and contempt for a social system that keeps one's nose to the proverbial grindstone perpetually. Still, it has been an adventurous and interesting experience.

Belfast, in the early 1900s, was by no means a paradise for the worker, especially the youngster who had finished his schooling and was preparing for industrial life. It was a privilege to be apprenticed to a trade. Most apprentices were indentured and parents were compelled to back this with a financial guarantee of good faith. Having lost both my parents, I also lost my opportunity of a trade. My first adventure in search of work took me into the linen trade. I managed to secure a job in a flax agent's store which brought me into contact with mills and factories. I started at four shillings a week, rising to six after I had been there two years.

Fifty years ago, spinning mills were little less than slave shops. Those were the days of 'sweating' and 'half-timers'. A child of twelve was allowed to work three days in a mill and three at school. A boy's wage for the three days was two shillings and a penny as an inducement to become a useful worker. He commenced work at 6 am and was finished at 6 pm. If he missed a day at work he was compelled to attend school two days as a punishment. Joseph Devlin MP managed eventually to put an end to this exploitation.

The two main trade unions in the linen industry were the flax dressers, or hecklers, and the linenlappers. The 'hecklers' were the most argumentative group of workers I ever mixed with in any industry. They had a custom of setting aside one 'berth' at their benches for a 'reader'. This man, instead of working at his trade, read the morning newspapers to his comrades. He was at no loss as his share of the work was covered by the rest of his mates.

With no sign of a wage increase, I thought it expedient to find some other more profitable employment. I was offered a job in the stereotyping department of the old *Ulster Echo*, in Royal Avenue, at treble the wages I was receiving in the yarn merchant's store. I jumped at the opportunity. I worked fifty-eight hours a week and considered myself in clover.

Here I mixed with compositors and printers who were well read and above the average in intelligence and so I was forced to study books and periodicals to keep pace with the conversation carried on during meal intervals. They were ardent politicians, too, yet during election periods tempers rarely developed. Printing in Belfast, at the beginning of the century, was a flourishing trade and gave employment to thousands of workers. Some of our best known artists held contracts with lithographical firms of international reputation for poster designs and colouring.

Shortly before World War I, I became tired of inside work and decided that an outside job would benefit my physical health, so I crossed the channel. Navvy work on railways and excavation pitches didn't suit me, nor tramping the English countryside in search of it. A pick seems a light enough tool for a novice, but after you have used it for an hour you reckon a sledgehammer is a child to it. In the old days, machinery was slow and cumbersome and often outpassed by manual labour. It was stubborn courage and brute strength that broke down Mother Nature's defence against the march of progress. I scuttled back home and picked up a job in the shipyards as a helper with the boilermakers. All my book lore, art studies and cultural outlook went up in smoke. Forty years ago in the shipyards life was raw, standards were crude and spoken English a revelation. This may all be changed now.

A shipyard labourer earned one pound a week in wages but you did get paid in coin of the realm. A golden sovereign was placed in your hand on payday. It's a 'wheen' of years since I've set eyes on a similar coin. You worked from 6 am till 5.30 pm, with a noon stop on Saturday. There was a forty-minute break for breakfast and an hour interval for dinner. The *Baltic, Celtic* and ill-fated *Titanic* were building then; the great gantries were still a nine-days wonder. Cantilevers were only beginning to lessen the labour of block and tackle. One had to bear a charmed life not to become a casualty 'out on the boats'.

The older boilermakers were a tough lot. When I first started in the yard, they were mostly riveters and used to 'piece work'. They balanced on rickety staging, wobbled across crazy gang planks and sent hot rivets flying through space in the hope they would land in firm ground rather than on the back of someone's neck.

You were no veteran in the shipyard until you bore a scar of some description about your body. I was hardly a month on the 'boats' when a seven-eight spanner came bouncing into the stoke-hole from the skylight above, bringing with it my first honourable wound. This was followed a year later by an iron wedge jumping out of some loose plates to leave a gash in my leg that kept me limping for days.

There were compensations for all this. The beauty and symmetrical lines of a finished liner steaming out to sea on its maiden voyage was symbolic of man's ingenuity; the glowing sunrise of an October morning glinting through the trellised structure of the gantries, to shape poetry out of an otherwise prosaic scene; the drama of men's lives around you which needed little observation to visualise; the tragedy and comedy of the everyday events of industrial life.

These things may not add to your material wealth or comforts but they do enrich your knowledge of life and bring you experiences that eventually broaden your outlook into an appreciation of the fact that you are living in a world which isn't just as ugly as some folk would have you believe.

Cornmarket

A Belfastman, or even a casual visitor to the city, is nearly bound to realise, by instinct if not knowledge, that this piece of ground carries a historical past going back to the earliest days of the town. The name itself would impress you with this fact. From the remotest times, when communities formed themselves into villages, there sprang up a castle for defence purposes, a church for worship, and a market for trading. Cornmarket had a similar beginning.

During the 17th century, the Donegall family presented the town with a market house, which stood at the corner of High Street and what is now Cornmarket. The market house practically faced the castle gates. The castle wall ran along one side of Cornmarket to Arthur Street, right up to which the waters of the River Lagan flowed at high tide. In fact the Lord of the Manor had his pleasure boat anchored there, convenient to the castle.

Cornmarket is mentioned in a lease for the year 1727. In the maps of the period, it is occasionally named 'The Shambles'. Actually, Cornmarket led to the Shambles, which was situated about where Arthur Street now stands. Round the middle of the 18th century, it is mentioned as 'Shambles

Street'. However, to the Belfast citizen of those days, it was the market square and here the housewives gossiped their heads off, and the town officials announced the warnings and regulations to the assembled townspeople.

In the 18th century, the well-to-do merchants built their Georgian houses and made the square a residential quarter, until the tradesmen, mostly butchers, squeezed these gentlemen out of their homes and forced them to rebuild their palaces in the vicinity of College Square and Donegall Place. Soon Cornmarket was the centre of Belfast. Besides being the shopping centre of the town, it was also used as the place for executions.

It was here, facing the market house, that Henry Joy McCracken walked bravely to the scaffold after the defeat of the United Irishmen at Antrim town in 1798. Not many yards distant was his home in 17 High Street, where his sister, Mary, was escorted after she had begged to be allowed to remain at his side till the last.

Here, too, in 1816, were brought from Carrick jail the two Peter's Hill weavers, sentenced to death for wrecking their employer's house in Millfield. This, perhaps, was the most cruel scene ever enacted there, the authorities actually carting the scaffold with its victims from Carrick, then, whilst the two condemned men stood by, building the crude structure in full view of both spectators and sufferers.

When the castle gates, facing the market house, were demolished and the ground built over in 1767, a new carriage way was made leading into Castle Lane. It was given the title of 'Hammond's Court' but, during the '70s of last century, the residents demanded a more respectable name and it became 'Castle Arcade', which it still retains. Here Sheridan Knowles, the famous Irish dramatist, conducted a school above one of the shops and, in 1824, Finlay printed his first issue of the radical *Northern Whig*.

The following year Grattans opened their shop in Cornmarket, and Marcus Ward, whose printing firm was to become world famous, opened another a few yards distant. The old market house was demolished in 1806, to be replaced later by Forster Green, the great tea merchants.

Meanwhile, Robert Montgomery, a lawyer, rented the ground upon which the castle had stood, and established a market for fish, fruit, meat and potatoes. The Corporation immediately took action against him for refusing to pay tolls, but Montgomery beat them in the courts, as the Castle grounds were exempt from all tolls according to custom. Castle market, or 'Montgomery's Market', as it was often referred to in my young days, retained its cobble-paved look until the Classic Cinema revolutionised the whole surroundings in 1921.

Today, Cornmarket is still a busy, thriving centre and, although many of its original concerns and shops have vanished, it still retains that traditional atmosphere that easily compels one to visualise its aspect a century and a half years ago.

Smithfield

Belfast is fast losing its connection with what we now refer to as 'Old Belfast'. Speech, customs and costumes, change so rapidly that one generation can soon lose all trace of how their fathers and mothers lived, how they clothed themselves, the type of entertainment they indulged in, what they drank and ate, the songs they sang and tunes they whistled, and even how they travelled from one place to another. But for the historians and artists placing on record in words and pictures the happenings of their day, one might even forget that the city had a beginning.

Still, we have an odd building that has survived the march of time, an odd district that retains some resemblance to what it appeared to our fathers and grandfathers. One such district is Smithfield, which looks much the same today as it did in my grandfather's day, a hundred years ago. Even then, it wasn't a great deal changed from *his* grandfather's time.

Smithfield was the first 'Commons', or open space, where the public could take a 'breather'. The entire town, at the time, was the property of Lord Donegall, which meant that he wasn't giving much away. When a Belfast merchant bought any land from His Lordship, in those days, he immediately fenced it in for future investment. Philanthropy was an unknown quality amongst our well-to-do citizens in the early days. There were no Dunvilles, Musgraves, or Barnetts, to add to the pleasure of the fellow citizens and, incidentally, preserve for the city a few acres of green pastures.

Whilst Donegall Place and its vicinity became the 'Rotten Row' of the aristocracy, Smithfield developed into a rendezvous of the working-class of the town. It became the market place, the fair ground, the playing fields for the weavers of Millfield and Mill Street during the early half of last century.

It has always been a square, an open space. Even when the town became an industrial area and factories and streets were springing up like mushrooms in a day, Smithfield retained its patch of green, where workers and their children whiled away whatever leisure hours were granted them from factory and mill.

Passing from a fair ground, Smithfield developed into a market place where pedlars and dealers displayed their wares. One can visualise half of the population of the town congregating here for a bargain, with gamesters and toughs seeking an easy method of making an odd shilling at the expense of their more simple townsfolk. When Smithfield was eventually roofed into a Corporation market, the hobby-horse, side-shows and boxing booth found another happy hunting ground in McCleans fields, at Ormeau Avenue which, in later years, received the popular title of the 'Chapel Fields'.

Round about the middle of last century, there was something like ten clothes dealers and eight auctioneers doing business in the Square. By this time, the new Town Council had taken over from the Sovereign and ruling Burgess, who were actually delegated to their positions by the Lord of the Manor, and Smithfield was, at last, a covered-in market. Previous to this, part of the square had been used as cattle pens. Tin smiths, coopers and booksellers also occupied stalls in the market.

Most of the public houses in the square were 'free and easies', supplying their customers with a song and dance as well as with pints. In opposition to the publicans was a 'Teetotal Hall', with a Pat McShane as superintendent. I think McShane eventually retired from the unequal contest as the hall disappears from the local directory, to give place to the Royal Hibernian Concert Hall which was, in fact, a typical Victorian music hall, under the management of Robert Calvert.,

The cultural outlook of the Smithfield people expressed itself during the same period in the support of a 'National Theatre', controlled by Tom Armstrong. The type of play produced was, naturally, inspired according to the charge of admission. The prices ranged from a penny to threepence, which must be considered quite moderate for a Shakespearean session. About 1864, a National School was established, to be followed shortly afterwards by a lending library.

Much could be added to this brief outline of the history of Smithfield and its square. It has outlived many of Belfast's older institutions. With the exception of Clifton House (1774) and the Linen Hall Library (1788), it is all that is left of old-time Belfast.

No doubt it will always hold a warm place in the hearts of Belfastmen no matter what place in the world they find themselves in.

The Romance of the Falls Road

When the Chichester family occupied the town of Belfast in the 17th century, they saw to it that no Irish place name would survive their overlordship. Tradition is hard to obliterate, and the inhabitants of the surrounding countryside held grimly to the ancient titles of their native townlands. So we have the oldest and central part of the city ornamented with the Christian and surnames of titled gentry and local merchants, whose pedigrees are as doubtful as their contributions to the progress of the town itself.

Still, it is a consolation to the Belfast citizen that we still retain such ancient titles as Stranmillis, Malone, Ormeau, Cromac, Shankill and the Falls. The influence of the Donegall family upon the Town Council during the 17th and 18th centuries encouraged their servitors to obliterate as far as possible all reference to the early origin of the various districts comprising the town.

Most of the earlier maps of Belfast refer to the Shankill as the Antrim Road, but once the new road to Antrim was constructed in the 1830s, the inhabitants insisted, by word of mouth, which has more authenticity than maps, in returning the district to its ancient origin. The Falls, which was the old highway to Dunmurry and Crumlin, never lost its traditional title in any single generation.

The powers that be at that period were satisfied to refer to the Falls simply as the road from Crumlin. To this day it remains the road from Crumlin.

Up till the early half of last century, the Falls had no real existence as a populated district. True, there were a few farms and labourer's cottages scattered about the hillsides where the mountainy people struggled hopelessly to earn a living on the poor and stony soil. With the exception of Andersonstown, where there was a small cluster of houses, the road was a bleak, unfrequented highway.

During the 1830s, the Falls Road commenced at Barrack Street and here a distillery was erected. Further along, where Dover Street now stands, a cotton factory was established and, a short distance above that, a flour mill commenced operations. The Falls had become industrialised! Barrack Street was still the limit of the town boundary and accommodation was limited outside this for workers, so that most of the employees of these new undertakings were recruited from Castle Street and Smithfield.

Hoping to include the new industries into a proposed extended boundary of the town, the Council pushed the Falls further into the countryside and re-named the thorougfare Mill Street. Later, they again changed the name to Divis Street, giving the Falls a further push back, this time to where Northumberland Street now stands. Then the Town Fathers ran out of names and were forced to allow the ancient Falls to retain its original meaning.

The Donegalls had, meanwhile, been deprived of their overlordship and had no say in the naming of thoroughfares.

In 1839, there was a linen factory, a flax mill and a bleach works, two private residences and a pub. By 1842, the public houses had increased to eight. There were now five flax spinning mills, a number of bleachers and linen manufacturers, with a flour mill and two dairies and private residences had, accordingly, increased in numbers. The Falls had developed into an industrial area.

It was in 1842 the opportunity came to the citizens to run the town according to their own wishes, and not to the whim of the Lord of the Manor. Lord Donegall's privately appointed Sovereign and Burgesses were replaced by an elected mayor and Town Council and immediately the borough took on an aspect of stedy progress. Streets began to take shape. Boundary Street, Hamilton Place, Ardmoulin Street, Bogan Street, Craig Street were constructed to house the workers. New industries in the form of a foundry and print works were established.

By the year 1856, the Falls was a built-up area. Conway Street, Norfolk Street, Alma, Balaklava, Sevastopol Streets, all named after battles of the Crimean War, were added to the list. Spinning mills were spearing the sky with their great chimney stacks and streets of small kitchen houses were spreading like mushrooms between the Shankill and the Falls.

The Shankill and the Falls! Two great communities growing up side by side, sharing their industrial tragedies and slackness and poverty together, knowing too well that what hurt one hurt the other, yet allowing themselves to be led into opposite channels of religious and political strife.

Sandwiched in between the two great thoroughfares were mills, factories and foundries that were adding much to the progress and richness of their home town, and, even today, the Falls and the Shankill seem to rival each other in extending their influence far beyond the original boundary where once they were mere names of outlying townlands on the map of Belfast.

The Shankill
—Road of the White Church

The average Belfast citizen approaching the Shankill Road rarely gives a thought to its historical origin, let alone its modern growth from an ancient townland into a great thoroughfare.

Shankill (the White Church) goes far back into antiquity. The old cemetery above Tennent Street is the site of the earliest church, as it was usual, even in olden times, to bury the dead in close proximity to ecclesiastical buildings. St. Matthew's Parish Church still retains the baptismal font of the first church; it was discovered by accident from some old ruins in the graveyard many years ago.

Sometime during the early part of the 14th century, the 'White Church' was erected in the grounds of the present cemetery, and travellers between mid-County Antrim and the ford, or crossing, at the mouth of the Farset River which made intercourse with County Down possible, would halt to seek a blessing from the Abbot of the White Church. Thus began what is now the Shankill Road. This was long before the highway between Dublin and Carrick, and Malone was a mere meadowland.

Eventually, towards the 16th century, this route for travellers through Shankill took shape and became something more than a beaten track. Wayfarers mounted and on foot, as well as farmers carting their produce from Antrim into the now growing town of Belfast, would cross the pass between Squire's Hill and Divis into the town. The road ran through a wilderness of moorland and rough, shrubby country until one came to Ballysillan where an occasional thatched cottage broke the monotony of heather and whin bushes.

It was during the later years of King William III's reign that the famous highwaymen, the O'Hagan brothers, crept from their hideout on Squire's Hill to maltreat and rob any rich merchant or unfortunate farmer who might use the Shankill or, as it was then called, the Antrim Road, without adequate escort.

The highwaymen became such a menace to travellers that the authorities detailed a squadron of dragoons to rid the district of these pests and they were eventually driven off to find new quarters on Knocknagh Mountain. From there they plied their nefarious trade upon rich merchants travelling between Carrick and Belfast.

Peter's Hill, which was the forerunner of the Shankill Road, is named on an old map of Belfast as being St. Peter's Hill and was in its early years a fashionable quarter of the town. As far back as 1823, there were as many as five hundred people living on the hill and, in nearby Brown Square, another one thousand and sixty.

When Donegall Place was constructed as a residential quarter of the town, in 1785, most of the rich merchants of Peter's Hill moved from that district and the handloom soon occupied the vacated houses.

It was at Brown Square that Jimmy Hope, the Templepatrick weaver, poet and '98 leader, finished the latter years of his life, although when he died, in 1843, he was laid to rest in Mallusk Cemetery, not far from his home town.

During Hope's lifetime, another Shankill Road labourer, Andrew MacKenzie, was publishing some notable verse in the local press. He died shortly after Hope and was buried in the old Shankill graveyard where a monument is erected to his memory.

The town boundary in the '40s of last century ran along Townsend Street which was, in fact, the end of the town and it was after a linen factory, distillery and the Soho foundry had been established in the neighbourhood of Brown Square that the Shankill really came into the town as the population moved up the steep incline of Bower's Hill, which stretched as far as Agnes Place.

M'Tier Street, Spear's Court and Conway Street soon appeared on the map, and a church was built at Argyle Place. By 1865, linen factories were functioning at Boundary Street and Conway Street. The Corporation had by now changed the title of 'lane', 'court' and 'place' to the more modern name of street, although in a few cases the old title remained.

When I was still a youth, the Shankill Road was sometimes referred to as Bower's Hill by the older generation. In fact, Bower's Hill bakery and Post Office were situated above Dover Street during the latter half of the last century. Woodvale House and estate, which stood above the cemetery on the left, gave the upper end of the road its name.

There is a similarity between the Shankill and Sandy Row in that both districts have been built up by working-class citizens.

Gentry and well-to-do merchants, even from the earliest days of the town's growth, gave both these thoroughfares a wide berth. Probably the great mills and factories, which sprang up between the Falls and the Shankill during the industrial progress of Belfast, were the chief cause of this.

Six hundred years ago, the Shankill was a barren wasteland with a rough track leading to the ford across the Lagan and an ancient church inviting the wayfarer to worship at its shrine as he passed on his way. A bare hundred years ago, it comprised a few cottages and farms here and there along its broadened carriageway.

Today, it is a densely populated district with its inhabitants feeding the mills, factories and shipyards with skilled labour. The ancient track has developed through the centuries into a great thoroughfare and banks, business offices and thriving merchants have made it one of the most progressive centres of Belfast.

There is a certain glamour attached to the Shankill, if one has the observant eye. As one approaches the rise of Peter's Hill on a clear summer afternoon, and casts an eye beyond to where the Shankill disappears over the steep incline of Bower's Hill into its Woodvale suburb, there is a grand view of Divis Mountain with its varied colours of golden corn, green field and purple heather, and an occasional white-washed cottage or farmhouse mirrored in the sunshine.

Thomas Carnduff
—a select bibliography

Correspondence

Mary Carnduff, c.150 letters from Thomas Carnduff 1940-1943
Theresa Lee, 7 letters from Thomas Carnduff dating from December 1937 to March 1940

Plays, including radio drama

'Birth of a giant' (broadcast by BBC December 1937—a collaboration with Denis Johnston.)
* 'Bluebeard' (typescript fragment for pantomime, 1937?)
'Castlereagh' (first performed at the Empire Theatre, 1935.)
* 'Curfew' (referred to in press in 1936 and in correspondence up to 1942. Carnduff's shorthand title for the project was 'Derry'.)
* 'The First Warrant' (a play in two acts, possibly dating from c.1930. Missing act two.)
'Give Losers Leave To Talk' (a Belfast shipyard play in three acts.)
* 'The Haunted House' (a one act farce, performed by York Street Non-Subscribing Presbyterian Church Dramatic Society, 1930.)
'Industry' (broadcast by the BBC, 1939.)
'Jonathan Swift'
'The Last Banshee' (a tragedy of County Antrim life in three acts.)
* 'Machinery' (first performed at the Abbey Theatre, 1933. Act three still missing.)
* 'Murder at the New Road' (broadcast on Radio Éireann, 1937, first written as 'Murder at Stranmillis'.)
* 'Politics' (performed by Stanhope Players, 1929.)
* 'Revolt in Ballyduff' (performed by York Street Non-Subscribing Presbyterian Church Dramatic Society, 1930.)
'Shipyardmen' (a one-act play for radion set in 1932.)
'The Stars Foretell' (reading given at the Young Ulster Society, 1938.)
'Traitors' (first performed at the Empire Theatre, 1934.)
'War Brides' (anti-war play dating from c. 1930?)
* 'The Wedding' (broadcast BBC)

* 'Workers' (first performed at the Abbey Theatre, 1932. Act one still missing.)
'The Young Jonathan Swift'

* Text either wholly lost or incomplete. Where text is available, either originals or copies are held by the Linen Hall Library.

Other radio scripts

'A Dustman's Life', BBC, July 1936.
'What town planning could do for me—a binman', BBC 1937.
'Northern Ireland contribution to Christmas Day Empire exchange, 1939', BBC.

Books

Carnduff, Thomas. *Poverty street and other poems*, Belfast, Lapwing Press 1993, 75pp
Carnduff, Thomas. *Songs from the shipyard and other poems*, Belfast, E.H. Thornton 1924, 47pp
Carnduff, Thomas. *Songs of an Out-of-Work*, Belfast, Quota Press 1932, 55pp
[Smyth, Denis] *Poet of the people: Thomas Carnduff 1886-1956*, a Belfast man, a brief story of his life, times and literary works, Belfast, North Belfast History Workshop 1991, unpaginated

Journal articles

Carnduff, Thomas: 'Belfast', in *The Bell*, Vol. IV No. 4 (July 1942), pp. 269-73 and No. 6 (September 1942), p. 456.
Carnduff, Thomas: 'Belfast is an Irish city', in *The Bell*, Vol. XVIII No. 1 (April 1952), pp. 5-7.
Carnduff, Thomas: 'I remember, being reminiscences of his life in Belfast', in *The Bell*, Vol. V No. 4 (January 1943), pp. 276-80.
Carnduff, Thomas: 'Orange Republican memoirs of Thomas Carnduff', in the *Irish Democrat*, March 1958, p. 7: April 1958, p. 7; May 1958, p. 7; June 1958, p. 7; July 1958, p. 9.
Carnduff, Thomas: 'The Orange Society', in *The Bell*, Vol. XVII No. 4 (July 1951), pp. 26-32.
Gray, John: 'Thomas Carnduff', in the *Linen Hall Review*, Vol. 3 No. 3

(Autumn 1986), p. 18.

Gray, John: 'Thomas Carnduff', 1886-1956: chapters from an unpublished autobiography', in *Irish Booklore*, Vol. 4 No. 1 (1978), pp. 24-26.

Newspaper articles

Thomas Carnduff wrote at least 150 articles and possibly as many as 200 for the press and almost as many may have been published with reference to him. One list available shows 60 articles published as early as March 1929. This and copies of the very many other cuttings available are held by the Linen Hall Library, albeit with the disadvantage that in most cases the cuttings concerned are undated and in many cases the identity of the publishing newspaper is not clear. This limits the value of any full bibliographical listing until further work has been done.